MY POLITICS EMAIL BOOK is a full array of HUNDREDS of political rhetoric and political issues; a collection of emails over the years; for your education, enlightenment and enjoyment. This book is not intended to offend anyone. It is my hope this book will open your eyes to information not covered by today's media and most folks don't wish to discuss. This book requires strength to face facts.

<u>RECOMMENDED FOR ADULT READERS</u>

ENJOY THIS READING

BRYAN CLARK

OIL - YOU BETTER SIT DOWN

More Stupidity from our Liberal Environmentalists...

Here's an interesting read, important and verifiable information: About 6 months ago, the writer was watching a news program on oil and one of the Forbes Bros. was the guest. The host said to Forbes, "I am going to ask you a direct question and I would like a direct answer; how much oil does the U.S. have in the ground?" Forbes did not miss a beat, he said, "more than all the Middle East put together." Please read below.

The U. S. Geological Service issued a report in April 2008 that only scientists and oil men knew was coming, but man was it big. It was a revised report (hadn't been updated since 1995) on how much oil was in this area of the western 2/3 of North Dakota , western South Dakota , and extreme eastern Montana...check THIS out:

The Bakken is the largest domestic oil discovery since Alaska's Prudhoe Bay, and has the potential to eliminate all American dependence on foreign oil. The Energy Information Administration (EIA) estimates it at 503 billion barrels. Even if just 10% of the oil is recoverable... at $107 a barrel, we're looking at a resource base worth more than $5.3 trillion.

"When I first briefed legislators on this, you could practically see their jaws hit the floor. They had no idea..." says Terry Johnson, the Montana Legislature's financial analyst.

"This sizable find is now the highest-producing onshore oil field found in the past 56 years," reports The Pittsburgh Post Gazette. It's a formation known as the Williston Basin, but is more commonly referred to as the 'Bakken.' It stretches from Northern Montana, through North Dakota and into Canada. For years, U. S. oil exploration has been considered a dead end. Even the 'Big Oil' companies gave up searching for major oil wells decades ago. However, a recent technological breakthrough has opened up the Bakken's massive reserves…and we now have access of 500 billion barrels. And because this is light, sweet oil, those billions of barrels will cost Americans just $16-per barrel!

That's enough crude to fully fuel the American economy for 2041 years straight. And if that didn't throw you on the floor, then this next one should - because it's from 2006!

U. S. Oil Discovery- Largest Reserve in the World Stansberry Report Online - 4/20/2006:

Hidden 1,000 feet beneath the surface of the Rocky Mountains lies the largest untapped oil reserve in the world. It is more than 2-trillion barrels. On August 8, 2005 President Bush mandated its extraction. In three and a half years of high oil prices none has been extracted. With this mother lode of oil why are we still fighting over off-shore drilling?

They reported this stunning news: We have more oil inside our borders than all the other proven reserves on earth. Here are the official estimates:

8-times as much oil as Saudi Arabia

18-times as much oil as Iraq

21-times as much oil as Kuwait

22-times as much oil as Iran

500-times as much oil as Yemen

And it's all right here in the Western United States.

How can this be? How can we not be extracting this? Because the Liberal environmentalists and others have blocked all efforts to help America become independent of foreign oil! Again, we are letting a small group of people dictate our lives and our economy...why? James Bartis, lead researcher with the study says we've got more oil in this very compact area than the entire Middle East -more than 2-trillion barrels untapped. That's more than all the proven oil reserves of crude oil in the world today, reports The Denver Post.

Don't think 'OPEC' will drop its price - even with this find? Think again!

It's all about the competitive marketplace, - it has to. Think OPEC just might be funding the environmentalists?

Got your attention yet? Now, while you're thinking about it, do this: Pass this along. If you don't take a little time to do this, then you should stifle yourself the next time you complain about gas prices – by doing nothing, you forfeit your right to complain.

Now I just wonder what would happen in this country if every one of you sent this to everyone in your address book.

By the way...this is all true. Check it out at the link below!

GOOGLE it...it will blow your mind.

http://www.usgs.gov/newsroom/article.asp?ID=1911

WHICH ONE ARE YOU?

If you have spent time in Washington:

Conservative...you are part of the problem

Liberal...you have experience

If you don't have time in Washington:

Conservative...you have no experience

Liberal…you represent change

If you have wealth:

Conservative …you are greedy and a cheat who had advantages in life

Liberal…you are successful and your life story is an inspiration

If you don't have wealth:

Conservative…you are low class

Liberal…you are disadvantaged

If you went to college:

Conservative…your academic pedigree is scrutinized

Liberal…your degree speaks for itself

If you didn't go to college:

Conservative…you are un-educated

Liberal…you are an artist/activist

If you own a business:

Conservative…you are a profiteer

Liberal…you provide jobs to the community

If you are working class:

Conservative…you're just a (insert job title or trade)

Liberal…you are a proletariat who finds strength in numbers

If you believe in the wisdom of the constitution:

Conservative…you are narrow minded

Liberal…you are a civil libertarian

If you believe in individual freedoms:

Conservative…you have made peace with inequality

Liberal...you are for choice

If you take to the streets to voice your opinions:

Conservative…you are a thug

Liberal…you are a demonstrator

If you are religious:

Conservative…you are a fundamentalist

Liberal…you are spiritual

If you are serving in the military:

Conservative…you are a mindless killer

Liberal…you wear the uniform of your country

If you are popular:

Conservative…you have blind sheep followers

Liberal…you are leading a movement

If you are attractive:

Conservative…you are shallow and empty

Liberal…you are stunning and a trend setter

If you are un-attractive:

Conservative…you are just ugly

Liberal…you are too intellectual to be concerned with your appearance

If you enjoy an outdoors lifestyle:

Conservative…you are a hick

Liberal…you are earthy

If you don't like guns:

Conservative…you don't buy one

Liberal…you want all guns outlawed

If you are a vegetarian:

Conservative…you don't eat meat

Liberal…you want all meat products banned for everyone

If you see a foreign threat:

Conservative…you think about how to defeat the enemy

Liberal…you wonder how to surrender gracefully and still look good

If you are a homosexual:

Conservative…you quietly lead your life

Liberal…you demand legislative respect

If you are black or hispanic:

Conservative…you see yourself as independently successful

Liberal…you see yourself as a victim in need of government protection

If you are down and out:

Conservative…you think about how to better your situation

Liberal…you wonder who is going to take care of you

If you don't like a talk show host:

Conservative…you switch channels

Liberal…you demand those you don't like be shut down

If you are a non-believer:

Conservative…you don't go to church

Liberal…you want any mention of God and religion silenced

If you need health care:

Conservative…you go about shopping for it, or may choose a job that provides it

Liberal…you demand that the rest of us pay for it

If you slip and fall in a store:

Conservative…you get up, laugh and are embarrassed

Liberal…you grab your neck, moan like you're in labor and then sue the store owner for negligence

If you read this:

Conservative…you will forward it so your friends can have a good laugh

Liberal…you will delete it because you feel "offended"

THE ONE

And it came to pass in the Age of Insanity that the people of the land called America, having lost their morals, their initiative, and their will to defend their liberties, chose as their Supreme Leader that person known as "the one."

He emerged from the vapors with a message that had no meaning; but He hypnotized the people telling them, "I am sent to save you." My lack of experience, my questionable ethics, my monstrous ego, and my association with evil doers are of no consequence. I shall save you with hope and change. Go, therefore, and proclaim throughout the land that he who preceded me is evil, that he has defiled the nation, and that all he has built must be destroyed. And the people rejoiced, for even though they knew not what "the one" would do, he had promised that it was good; and they believed. And "the one" said " We live in the greatest country in the world. Help me change everything about it!" And the people said, "Hallelujah! Change is good!"

Then He said, "We are going to tax the rich fat-cats." And the people said "Sock it to them!" "And redistribute their wealth." And the people said, "Show us the money!" And then he said, "Redistribution of wealth is good for everybody."

And Joe the plumber asked, "Are you kidding me? You're going to steal my money and give it to the deadbeats??" And "the one" ridiculed and taunted him, and Joe's personal records were hacked and publicized.

One lone reporter asked, "Isn't that Marxist policy?" And she was banished from the kingdom!

Then a citizen asked, "with no foreign relations experience and having zero military experience or knowledge, how will we deal with radical terrorists?" And "the one" said, "Simple. I shall sit with them and talk with them and show them how nice we really are; and they will forget that they ever wanted to kill us all!" And the people said, "Hallelujah!! We are safe at last, and we can beat our weapons into free cars for the people!"

Then "the one" said "I shall give 95% of you lower taxes." And one, lone voice said, "But 40% of us don't pay any taxes." So "The One" said, "Then I shall give you some of the taxes the fat-cats pay!" And the people said, "Hallelujah! Show us the money!"

Then "the one" said, "I shall tax your Capital Gains when you sell your homes!" And the people yawned and the slumping housing market collapsed. And He said. "I shall mandate employer-funded health care for every worker and raise the minimum wage. And I shall give every person unlimited healthcare and medicine and transportation to the Clinics." And the people said, "Give me some of that!"

Then he said, "I shall penalize employers who ship jobs overseas." And the people said, "Where's my rebate check?"

Then "The One" said, "I shall bankrupt the coal industry and electricity rates will skyrocket!" And the people said, "Coal is dirty, coal is evil, no more coal! But we don't care for that part about higher electric rates."

So "The One" said, not to worry. "If your rebate isn't enough to cover your expenses, we shall bail you out. Just sign up with ACORN and you troubles are over!"

Then He said, "Illegal immigrants feel scorned and slighted. Let's grant them amnesty, Social Security, free education, free lunches, free medical care and bi-lingual signs and guaranteed housing..."

And the people said, "Hallelujah!" and they made him king!

And so it came to pass that employers, facing spiraling costs and ever-higher taxes, raised their prices and laid off workers. Others simply gave up and went out of business and the economy sank like unto a rock dropped from a cliff.

The banking industry was destroyed. Manufacturing slowed to a crawl. And more of the people were without a means of support.

Then "The One" said, "I am the "the One"- The Messiah - and I'm here to save you! We shall just print more money so everyone will have enough!" But our foreign trading partners said unto Him. "Wait a minute. Your dollar is not worth a pile of camel dung! You will have to pay more... And "The One" said, "Wait a minute. That is unfair!!" And the world said, "Neither are these other idiotic programs you have embraced. Lo, you have become a Socialist state and a second-rate power. Now you shall play by our rules!"

And the people cried out, "Alas, alas!! What have we done?" But yea verily, it was too late. The people set upon The One and spat upon him and stoned him, and his name was dung. And the once mighty nation was no more; and the once proud people were without sustenance or shelter or hope. And the Change "The One" had given them was as like unto a poison that had destroyed them and like a whirlwind that consumed all that they had built.

And the people beat their chests in despair and cried out in anguish, "give us back our nation and our pride and our hope!!" But it was too late, and their homeland was no more.

You may think this a fairy tale, but it's not.

It's happening right now!

HOW TO FIX THE ECONOMY

Dear "Mr." President:

Please find below my suggestion for fixing America's economy. Instead of giving billions of dollars to companies that will squander the money on lavish parties and unearned bonuses, use the following plan; I call it the Patriotic Retirement Plan.

There are about 40 million people over 50 in the work force. Pay them each $1 million severance for early retirement with the following stipulations:

1) They must retire. Forty million new job openings - unemployment fixed.

2) They must buy a new American car. Forty million cars ordered - auto industry fixed.

3) They must either buy a house or pay off their mortgage - Housing Crisis fixed.

It can't get any easier than that! If more money is needed, have all members of Congress reduce their income and pay higher taxes with

Term Limits.

If you agree that this would work, please implement this plan effective immediately.

If not, please shoot yourself!!!! This too would create a new job opening.

'URINE OR YOU'RE OUT'

Most folks in this country have a job. They work and they receive a paycheck. These people pay their taxes and their government distributes those taxes as it sees fit.

In order to receive that paycheck, most of these folks are required to pass a random urine/drug test, with which most working people have no problem. The problem exists with the distribution of these taxes to people who don't have to pass a similar test.

Question: Shouldn't one have to pass a urine test to get a welfare check, because these working people have to pass one to earn it for them?

Please understand, I have no problem with helping people get back on their feet or to help them in their time of need for a specified time period. I do, on the other hand, have a problem with helping someone sitting on their ass - doing drugs and getting drunk on my dime while I work.

Can you imagine how much money would be saved if these people had to pass a urine/drug test to get a public assistance check?

I guess we could title this program 'urine or you're out'.

I'll save you the trouble… this *IS* intended to be as mean spirited as it appears. It is my desire to afflict as much pain and shame to these people's 'feelings' as I possibly can. How about the inner-city 18-year old single mother of four children fathered by four different males who is about as uneducated as the day she was born in the jungle she lives in; but holds the right to 'vote'? How about these government handout recipients receiving their 'government checks' on the 3rd and 4th day of the month, cashing them and then buy their drugs and liquor and then be 'broke' 2-days later for the rest of the month and who also hold the right to 'vote'. Keep voting Democrat….These poor monkey baboons have been voting Democrat for the past 60-years and they're still poor monkey baboons. The government workings of the fine city of Detroit and the entire state of Michigan should be the only example you need. But don't forget about the 15-million illegals in this country that are on the verge of receiving these same 'entitlements'.

FAILURE

Addressed to all 535 voting members of the United States Legislature:

1) It is now official: You are all unfit for your elected representation.

2) The U.S. Postal Service was established in 1775 - you have had 234 years to get it right; and it is broke.

3) Social Security was established in 1935 - you have had 74 years to get it right; and it is broke.

4) Fannie Mae was established in 1938 - you have had 71 years to get it right; and it is broke.

5) War on Poverty started in 1964 - you have had 45 years to get it

right; $1 trillion of our money is confiscated each year and transferred to "the poor"; it hasn't worked, doesn't work and won't ever work!!

6) People who don't contribute into "the system" should not hold the right to vote for the idiots who run "the system". Try going to a bank to withdraw funds without ever making a deposit. Why are these entitlement receiving fools allowed to vote? Try justifying this point!

7) Medicare and Medicaid were established in 1965 - you've had 44 years to get it right; and they're both broke.

8) Freddie Mac was established in 1970 - you have had 39 years to get it right; and it is broke.

9) Trillions of dollars in the Massive political payoff called the "tarp bill of 2009" shows no sign of working.

10) And finally to set a new record: "Cash for Clunkers" was established in 2009 and went broke in 2009! It took good dependable cars (the best some people could afford) and replaced them with mostly high priced Japanese models so a good percentage of the profits from the sales went out of the country – good call!!. Most of these "new car buyers" couldn't afford a monthly car payment and now have a new payment!

11) And lastly, the American taxpayers are now going to be dinged with paying for yet 100's of billions/trillions more dollars of our government's experiments to make our wallets even thinner.

This factually proves that "services" you shove down our throats generate massive failure. Now you expect taxpaying and health insured Americans to believe you can be trusted with a government-run health care system that represents 15% of our economy? You have lost whatever mind you thought you had!!!! Truly, and excuse the cliché, the inmates are running the asylum! And what does this say about the dumbass voters who put these criminals in office? Maybe we need to let others in on this brilliant record before the 2010 mid-term elections and just vote against incumbents. Some people think we'd be better off electing the first <u>535</u> names in the phonebook.

OBAMA'S FIRST SIX MONTHS' ACCOMPLISHMENTS

1) Offended the Queen of England.

2) Bowed to the King of Saudi Arabia.

3) Praised the Marxist Daniel Ortega.

4) Kissed Socialist Hugo Chavez on the cheek.

5) Endorsed the Socialist Evo Morales of Bolivia.

6) Sided with Hugo Chavez and Communist Fidel Castro against Honduras.

7) Announced we would meet with Iranians with no pre-conditions while they're building their nuclear weapons.

8) Gave away billions to AIG also without pre-conditions.

9) Expanded the bailouts.

10) Insulted everyone who has ever loved a Special Olympian.

11) Doubled our national debt.

12) Announced the termination of our new missile defense system the day after North Korea launched an ICBM.

13) Released information on U.S. intelligence gathering despite urgings of his own CIA director and the prior four CIA directors.

14) Accepted without comment that five of his cabinet members cheated on their taxes and two other nominees withdrew after they couldn't take the heat.

15) Appointed a Homeland Security Chief who identified military veterans and abortion opponents as "dangers to the nation."

16) Ordered that the word "terrorism" no longer be used and instead refers to such acts as "man made disasters."

17) Circled the globe to publicly apologize for America 's world leadership.

18) Told the Mexican president that the violence in their country was because of us.

19) Politicized the census by moving it into the White House from the Department of Commerce.

20) Appointed as Attorney General the man who orchestrated the forced removal and expulsion to Cuba of a 9-year-old whose mother died trying to bring him to freedom in the United States.

21) Salutes as heroes three Navy SEALS who took down three terrorists who threatened one American life and the next day announces members of the Bush administration may stand trial for "torturing" three 9/11 terrorists by pouring water up their noses.

22) Low altitude photo shoot of Air Force One over New York City that frightened hundreds of thousands of New Yorkers.

23) Sent his National Defense Adviser to Europe to assure them that the US will no longer treat Israel in a special manner and they might be on their own with the Muslims.

24) Praised Jimmy Carter's trip to Gaza where he sided with terrorist

Hamas against Israel .

25) Nationalized General Motors and Chrysler while turning shareholder control over to the unions and freezing out retired investors who owned their bonds. Committed unlimited taxpayer billions in the process.

26) Passed a huge energy tax in the House that will make American industry even less competitive while costing homeowners thousands per year.

27) Announced nationalized health care "reform" that will strip seniors of their Medicare, cut pay of physicians, increase taxes yet another $1 trillion, and put everyone on rationed care with government bureaucrats deciding who gets care and who doesn't. Bloomberg: Daschle says, "Health care reform will not be pain free. Seniors should be more accepting of the conditions that come with age instead of treating them," while former Colorado Governor Dick Lamm says seniors have "a duty to die."

If this does not sufficiently raise your ire, just remember that the President, Senators and Congressmen have their own special gold plated health care plan which is guaranteed the remainder of their lives and they are not subject to this new law if they pass it.

Please use the power of the Internet to get this message out. Talk it up at the grassroots level. We have an election coming up in one year and four months where we can reverse the dangerous direction of the Obama administration and its allies. In the interim, we can make their lives miserable. Let's do it!

NEW DIVORCE AGREEMENT

Dear American Liberals, leftists, social progressives, socialists, Marxists and Obama supporters, et al:

We have stuck together since the late 1950's, but the whole of this latest election process has made me realize that I want a divorce. I know we tolerated each other for many years for the sake of future generations, but sadly, this relationship has run its course. Our two ideological sides of America cannot and will not ever agree on what is right so let's just end it on friendly terms.

We can smile and chalk it up to irreconcilable differences and go our own way.

HERE IS A MODEL SEPARATION AGREEMENT:

1) Our two groups can equitably divide up the country by landmass each taking a portion. That will be the difficult part, but I am sure our two sides can come to a friendly agreement. After that, it should be relatively easy! Our respective representatives can effortlessly divide other assets since both sides have such distinct and disparate tastes.

2) We don't like re-distributive taxes so you can keep them

3) You are welcome to the Liberal judges and the ACLU

4) Since you hate guns and war, we'll take our firearms, the cops, the NRA and the military. You can keep Oprah, Michael Moore and Rosie O' Donnell (You are, however, responsible for finding a bio-diesel vehicle big enough to move all three of them)

5) We'll keep the capitalism, greedy corporations, pharmaceutical companies, Wal-Mart and Wall Street. You can have your beloved homeless, homeboys, hippies and illegal aliens

6) We'll keep the hot Alaskan hockey moms, greedy CEO's and

rednecks. We'll keep the Bibles and give you NBC, ABC, CBS, SNBC, CNN and Hollywood

7) You can make nice with Iran and Palestine and we'll retain the right to invade and hammer places that threaten us

8) We'll continue to follow Ronald Reagan's motto of Peace Through Strength because we know how that sickens you

9) You can have the peaceniks 'and war protesters. When our allies or our way of life are under assault, we'll help provide them security

10) We'll keep our Judeo-Christian values. You are welcome to Islam, Scientology, Humanism and Shirley McClain. You can also have the U.N.. but we will no longer be paying the bill

11) Take Barbara Streisand & Jane Fonda with you

12) We'll keep the SUVs, pickups and oversized luxury cars. You can give everyone healthcare if you can find any practicing doctors. We'll continue to believe healthcare is a luxury and not a right

13) We'll keep The Battle Hymn of the Republic and the National Anthem. I'm sure you'll be happy to substitute Imagine, I'd Like to Teach the World to Sing, Kum Ba Ya or We Are the World

14) We'll practice trickledown economics and you can give trickle up poverty your best shot

15) Since it often so offends you, we'll keep our history, Praise to God and our flag

Would you agree to this? If so, please pass it along to other like minded Liberal and Conservative patriots and if you do not agree, just hit delete. In the spirit of friendly parting, I'll bet you ANWAR which one of us will need whose help in 15 years

---

HONORING THE DEPARTED

This is so sad and shows what we value!

Ed McMahon died. He was a great entertainer, but prior to his stage accomplishments he was a distinguished Marine Corps fighter pilot in WWII, earning six air medals and attaining the rank of Colonel. He was discharged in 1946 and was later promoted to the rank of Brigadier General in the California Air National Guard.

Farrah Fawcett died. After she was diagnosed with cancer, she became an activist for cancer treatment and devoted her remaining years encouraging people to seek treatment. She documented her plight on film and used it to encourage others to stay positive and upbeat despite their diagnosis and suffering.

Michael Jackson died. He was known to some as a great singer for modern time. He will also be remembered for his eccentric lifestyle that included sleeping with a chimpanzee, living in a carnival-like atmosphere at Neverland, his fascination with Peter Pan, and his numerous masks and costumes. He also admitted to finding pleasure sleeping with young boys and paying out millions of dollars in settlements to the families of these boys despite being acquitted by a court on one allegation of sexual molestation. Also, many other weird manifestations.

All three died within 2-weeks of each other

Question - Which of the above did the House of Representatives declare a moment of silence for last week? (Hint - it wasn't the first two.)

Question - Which of the above's family received a personal note of condolence from President Obama? (Hint - It wasn't the first two.) need we say more?

STIMULUS PLAN

This year, taxpayers will receive an Economic Stimulus Payment. This is a very exciting new program that I will explain using the Q and A format:

Q. What is an Economic Stimulus Payment?

A. It is money that the federal government will send to taxpayers

Q. Where will the government get this money?

A. From taxpayers

Q. So the government is giving me back my own money?

A. Only a smidgen

Q. What is the purpose of this payment?

A. The plan is that you will use the money to purchase a high-definition TV set, thus stimulating the economy

Q. But isn't that stimulating the economy of China?

A. Shut up

Below is some helpful advice on how to best help the US economy by spending your stimulus check wisely:

1) If you spend that money at Wal-Mart, all the money will go to China

2) If you purchase fruit and vegetables it will go to Mexico, Honduras, and Guatemala (unless you buy organic)

3) If you buy a car it will go to Japan

4) If you purchase useless crap it will also go to Taiwan.

5) And none of it will help the American economy.

6) We need to keep that money here in America. You can keep the money in America by spending it at yard sales, going to a baseball game, or spend it on prostitutes, beer (domestic only), or tattoos, since those are the only businesses still in the US.

Why not let us keep the money we give the government every month from our income, jobs, pensions and IRA's? It would cut out printing checks and mailing.

IT WAS 1987

It was 1987! At a lecture the other day they were playing an old news video of Lt. Col. Oliver North testifying at the Iran-Contra hearings during the Reagan Administration.

There was Ollie in front of God and country getting the third degree, but what he said was stunning! He was being drilled by a senator; 'Did you not recently spend close to $60,000 for a home security system?' Ollie replied, 'Yes, I did, Sir.' The senator continued, trying to get a laugh out of the audience 'Isn't that just a little excessive?' 'No, sir,' continued Ollie. 'No? And why not?' the senator asked. 'Because the lives of my family and I were threatened, sir.'

'Threatened? By whom?' the senator questioned. 'By a terrorist, sir' Ollie answered. 'Terrorist? What terrorist could possibly scare you that much?' 'His name is Osama bin Laden, sir' Ollie replied. At this point the senator tried to repeat the name, but couldn't pronounce it, which most people back then probably couldn't. A couple of people laughed at the attempt. Then the senator continued. Why are you so afraid of this man?' the senator asked. 'Because, sir, he is the most evil person alive that I know of', Ollie answered.

'And what do you recommend we do about him?' asked the senator. 'Well, sir, if it was up to me, I would recommend that an assassin team be formed to eliminate him and his men from the face of the earth.' The senator disagreed with this approach, and that was all that was shown of the clip.

By the way...that senator was Al Gore!

Also:

Terrorist pilot Mohammad Atta blew up a bus in Israel in 1986. The Israelis captured, tried and imprisoned him. As part of the Oslo agreement with the Palestinians in 1993, Israel had to agree to release so-called 'political prisoners.' However, the Israelis would not release any with blood on their hands, The American President at the time, Bill Clinton, and his Secretary of State, Warren Christopher, 'insisted' that all prisoners be released. Thus Mohammad Atta was freed and eventually thanked us by flying an airplane into Tower One of the World Trade Center...This was reported by many of the American TV networks at the time that the terrorists were first identified. It was censored in the U.S. from all later reports. If you agree that the American public should be made aware of this fact, pass this on.

PELOSI

FACTS:

Speaker of the House Nancy Pelosi's home House District includes San Francisco. Star-Kist Tuna's headquarters are in San Francisco,

Pelosi's home district. Star-Kist is owned by Del Monte Foods and is a major contributor to Pelosi.

Star-Kist is the major employer in American Samoa employing 75% of the Samoan workforce. Paul Pelosi, Nancy's husband, owns $17 million dollars of Star-Kist stock.

In January, 2007 when the minimum wage was increased from $5.15 to $7.25, Pelosi had American Samoa exempted from the increase so Del Monte would not have to pay the higher wage. This would make Del Monte products less expensive than their competition's.

Last week when the huge bailout bill was passed, Pelosi added an earmark to the final bill adding $33 million dollars for an "economic development credit in American Samoa".

Pelosi has called the Bush Administration "corrupt". She should know.'

THE "545" PEOPLE WHO ARE RUINING OUR COUNTRY

Read the following and then really think about our current political debacle:

Politicians are the only people in the world who create problems and then campaign against them.

Have you ever wondered why, "if both the Democrats and the Republicans are against deficits, why do we have deficits?"

Have you ever wondered why, "if all the politicians are against inflation and high taxes, why do we have inflation and high taxes?"

You and I don't propose a federal budget. The president does.

You and I don't have the Constitutional authority to vote on appropriations. The House of Representatives does.

You and I don't write the tax code, Congress does.

You and I don't set fiscal policy, Congress does.

You and I don't control monetary policy, the Federal Reserve Bank does.

One hundred Senators, 435 Congressmen, one president, and nine Supreme Court justices = 545 human beings out of the 300 million that are directly, legally, morally, and individually responsible for the domestic problems that plague this country.

I excluded the members of the Federal Reserve Board because that problem was created by the Congress. In 1913, Congress delegated its Constitutional duty to provide a sound currency to a federally chartered, but private, central bank.

I excluded all the special interests and lobbyists for a sound reason. They have no legal authority. They have no ability to coerce a senator, a Congressman, or a president to do one cotton-picking thing. I don't care if they offer a politician $1 million dollars in cash. The politician has the power to accept or reject it. No matter what the lobbyist promises, it is the legislator's responsibility to determine how he votes.

Those 545 human beings spend much of their energy convincing you that what they did is not their fault. They cooperate in this common con regardless of party.

What separates a politician from a normal human being is an excessive amount of gall. No normal human being would have the gall of a Speaker, who stood up and criticized the President for creating deficits. The president can only propose a budget. He cannot force the Congress to accept it.

The Constitution, which is the supreme law of the land, gives sole responsibility to the House of Representatives for originating and approving appropriations and taxes. Who is the speaker of the House? Nancy Pelosi. She is the leader of the majority party. She and fellow House members, not the president, can approve any budget they want. If the president vetoes it, they can pass it over his veto if they agree to.

It seems inconceivable to me that a nation of 300 million cannot replace 545 people who stand convicted -- by present facts -- of incompetence and irresponsibility. I can't think of a single domestic problem that is not traceable directly to those 545 people. When you fully grasp the plain truth that 545 people exercise the power of the federal government, then it must follow that what exists is what they want to exist.

If the tax code is unfair, it's because they want it unfair.

If the budget is in the red, it's because they want it in the red .

If the Army & Marines are in IRAQ , it's because they want them in IRAQ.

If they do not receive social security but are on an elite retirement plan not available to the people, it's because they want it that way. There are no insoluble government problems.

Do not let these 545 people shift the blame to bureaucrats, whom they hire and whose jobs they can abolish; to lobbyists, whose gifts and advice they can reject; to regulators, to whom they give the power to regulate and from whom they can take this power. Above all, do not let them con you into the belief that there exists disembodied mystical forces like "the economy," "inflation," or

"politics" that prevent them from doing what they take an oath to do.
Those 545 people, and they alone, are responsible.

They, and they alone, have the power.

They, and they alone, should be held accountable by the people who are their bosses. Provided the voters have the gumption to manage their own employees.

We should vote all of them out of office and clean up their mess!
What you do with this article now that you have read it is up to you, though you appear to have several choices:

1) You can send this to everyone in your address book, and hope "they" do something about it.

2) You can agree to "vote against" everyone that is currently in office, knowing that the process will take several years.

3) You can decide to "run for office" yourself and agree to do the job properly.

4) Lastly, you can sit back and do nothing, or re-elect the current bunch.

CHANGE...CHICAGO STYLE

Body count in the last six months 292 killed (murdered) in Chicago

Body count killed in Iraq same time period = 221.

United States Senators Obama and Dick Durbin

Congressman Jesse Jackson Jr.

Governor Rod Blogojevich

State House Leader Mike Madigan

Attorney General Lisa Madigan (daughter of Mike)

Mayor Richard M. Daley (son of former Mayor Richard J. Daley)

The entire leadership in Illinois.....all 'Democrats' (or... left wing fanatical ideologues)

Chicago is a combat zone, and of course, they're all blaming each other.

Can't blame Republicans... there aren't any!

State pension fund $44 Billion in debt, worst in country.

Cook County (Chicago) sales tax 10.25% highest in country. (Look 'em up if you want).

Chicago school system one of the worst in country.

This is the political culture that Obama comes from in Illinois.

And Obama is going to 'fix' Washington politics?

OBAMA'S NOT EXACTLIES

This guy is the slickest liar to come along yet. Bill and Hillary can't even begin to compete.

1) Selma Got Me Born - NOT EXACTLY, your parents felt safe enough to have you in 1961 - Selma had no effect on your birth, as Selma was in 1965. (Goggle 'Obama Selma' for his full March 4, 2007 speech and articles about its various untruths.)

2) Father was a goat herder - NOT EXACTLY, he was a privileged, well educated youth, who went on to work with the Kenyan Government.

3) Father Was A Proud Freedom Fighter - NOT EXACTLY, he was part of one of the most corrupt and violent governments Kenya has ever had.

4) My Family Has Strong Ties To African Freedom - NOT EXACTLY, your cousin Raila Odinga has created mass violence

in attempting to overturn a legitimate election in 2007, in Kenya. It is the first widespread violence in decades. The current government is pro-American but Odinga wants to overthrow it and establish Muslim Sharia law. Your half-brother, Abongo Obama, is Odinga's follower. You interrupted your New Hampshire campaigning to speak to Odinga on the phone. Check out the following link for verification of that....and for more. Obama's cousin Odinga in Kenya ran for president and tried to get Sharia Muslim law in place there. When Odinga lost the elections, his followers have burned Christians' homes and then burned men, women and children alive in a Christian church where they took shelter. Obama supported his cousin before the election process here started. Goggle Obama and Odinga and see what you get. No one wants to know the truth.

5) My Grandmother Has Always Been A Christian - NOT EXACTLY, she does her daily Salat prayers at 5 AM, according to her own interviews. Not to mention, Christianity wouldn't allow her to have been one of 14 wives to 1 man.

6) My Name is African Swahili - NOT EXACTLY, your name is Arabic and 'Baraka' (from which Obama came) means 'blessed' in that language. Hussein is also Arabic and so is Obama. Obama Hussein Obama is not half black. If elected, he would be the first Arab-American President, not the first black President. Obama Hussein Obama is 50% Caucasian from his mother's side and 43.75% Arabic and 6.25% African Negro from his father's side. While Obama Hussein Obama's father was from Kenya, his father's family were mainly Arabs. Obama Hussein Obama's

father was only 12.5% African Negro and 87.5% Arab (his father's birth certificate even states he's Arab, not African Negro).

7) I Never Practiced Islam - NOT EXACTLY, you practiced it daily at school, where you were registered as a Muslim and kept that faith for 31 years, until your wife made you change, so you could run for office.   4-3-08 Article 'Obama was 'quite religious in Islam's'.

8) My School In Indonesia Was Christian - NOT EXACTLY, you were registered as Muslim there and got in trouble in Koranic Studies for making faces (check your own book). February 28, 2008. Kristoff from the New York Times a year ago: Mr. Obama recalled the opening lines of the Arabic call to prayer, reciting them with a first-rate accent. In a remark that seemed delightfully uncalculated (it'll give Alabama voters heart attacks), Mr. Obama described the call to prayer as 'one of the prettiest sounds on Earth at sunset.' This is just one example of what Pamela is talking about when she says 'Obama's narrative is being altered, enhanced and manipulated to whitewash troubling facts.'

9) I Was Fluent In Indonesian - NOT EXACTLY, not one teacher says you could speak the language.

10) Because I Lived In Indonesia, I Have More Foreign Experience - NOT EXACTLY, you were there from the ages of 6 to 10, and couldn't even speak the language. What did you learn? How to study the Koran and watch cartoons.

11) I Am Stronger On Foreign Affairs - NOT EXACTLY, except for

Africa (surprise) and the Middle East (bigger surprise), you have never been anywhere else on the planet and thus have NO experience with our closest allies.

12) I Blame My Early Drug Use On Ethnic Confusion - NOT EXACTLY, you were quite content in high school to be Barry Obama, no mention of Kenya and no mention of struggle to identify - your classmates said you were just fine.

13) An Ebony Article Moved Me To Run For Office - NOT EXACTLY, Ebony has yet to find the article you mention in your book. It doesn't, and never did, exist.

14) A Life Magazine Article Changed My Outlook On Life - NOT EXACTLY, Life has yet to find the article you mention in your book. It doesn't, and never did, exist.

15) I Won't Run On A National Ticket In '08 - NOT EXACTLY, here you are, despite saying, live on TV, that you would not have enough experience by then, and you are all about having experience first.

16) Voting 'Present' is Common In Illinois Senate - NOT EXACTLY, they are common for YOU, but not many others have 130 no votes.

17) Oops, I Miss-voted - NOT EXACTLY, only when caught by church groups and Democrats, did you beg to change your miss-vote.

18) I Was A Professor Of Law - NOT EXACTLY, you were a senior lecturer on leave.

19) I Was A Constitutional Lawyer - NOT EXACTLY, you were a senior lecturer on leave.

20) Without Me, There Would Be No Ethics Bill - NOT EXACTLY, you didn't write it, introduce it, change it, or create it.

21) The Ethics Bill Was Hard To Pass - NOT EXACTLY, it took just 14 days from start to finish.

22) I Wrote A Tough Nuclear Bill - NOT EXACTLY, your bill was rejected by your own party for its pandering and lack of all regulation - mainly because of your Nuclear donor, Exelon, from which David Axelrod came.

23) I Have Released My State Records - NOT EXACTLY, as of March, 2008, state bills you sponsored or voted for have yet to be released, exposing all the special interests pork hidden within.

24) I Took On The Asbestos Altgeld Gardens Mess - NOT EXACTLY, you were part of a large group of people who remedied Altgeld Gardens. You failed to mention anyone else but yourself, in your books.

25) My Economics Bill Will Help America - NOT EXACTLY, your 111 economic policies were just combined into a proposal which lost 99-0, and even you voted against your own bill.

26) I Have Been A Bold Leader In Illinois - NOT EXACTLY, even your own supporters claim to have not seen BOLD action on your part.

27) I Passed 26 Of My Own Bills In One Year - NOT EXACTLY, they were not your bills, but rather handed to you, after their creation by a fellow Senator, to assist you in a future bid for higher office.

28) No One on my campaign contacted Canada about NAFTA - NOT EXACTLY, the Canadian Government issued the names

and a memo of the conversation your campaign had with them.

29) I Am Tough On Terrorism - NOT EXACTLY, you missed the Iran Resolution vote on terrorism and your good friend Ali Abunimah supports the destruction of Israel.

30) I Want All Votes To Count - NOT EXACTLY, you said let the delegates decide.

31) I Want Americans To Decide - NOT EXACTLY, you prefer caucuses that limit the vote, confuse the voters, force a public vote, and only operate during small windows of time.

32) I passed 900 Bills in the State Senate - NOT EXACTLY, you passed 26, most of which you didn't write yourself.

33) I Believe In Fairness, Not Tactics - NOT EXACTLY, you used tactics to eliminate Alice Palmer from running against you.

34) I Don't Take PAC Money - NOT EXACTLY, you take loads of it.

35) I don't Have Lobbyists - NOT EXACTLY, you have over 47 lobbyists, and counting.

36) My Campaign Had Nothing To Do With The 1984 Ad - NOT EXACTLY, your own campaign worker made the ad on his Apple in one afternoon.

37) I Have Always Been Against Iraq - NOT EXACTLY, you weren't in office to vote against it and you have voted to fund it every single time.

38) I Have Always Supported Universal Health Care – NOT EXACTLY, your plan leaves us all to pay for the 15,000,000 who don't have to buy it.

Please forward to all in your address book.

The truth must be known – EXACTLY

YOUR SOCIAL SECURITY

Just in case some of you young whippersnappers (& some older ones) didn't know this, be sure and show it to your "Democratic" friends and your kids. They need a little history lesson on what's what. And it doesn't matter whether you are Democrat of Republican. Facts are facts!!!

<u>Franklin Roosevelt</u>, a Democrat, introduced the Social Security (FICA) Program. He promised:

1) That participation in the Program would be completely voluntary

2) That the participants would only have to pay 1% of the first $1,400 of their annual incomes into the Program

3) That the money the participants elected to put into the Program would be deductible from their income for tax purposes each year

4) That the money the participants put into the Independent 'Trust Fund' rather than into the General Operating Fund, and therefore, would only be used to fund the Social Security Retirement Program, and no other government program

5) That the annuity payments to the retirees would never be taxed as income

6) Since many of us have paid into FICA for years and are now receiving a Social Security check every month -- and then finding that we are getting taxed on 85% of the money we paid to the federal government to 'put away', you may be interested in the following:

Q: Which political party took Social Security from the Independent

'Trust Fund' and put it in to the General Fund so that Congress could spend it?

A: It was Lyndon Johnson and the Democratically- controlled House and Senate

Q: Which political party eliminated the income tax deduction for Social Security (FICA) withholding?

A: The Democratic Party.

Q: Which political party started taxing Social Security annuities?

A: The Democratic Party, with Al Gore casting the 'tie-breaking' deciding vote as President of the Senate, while he was Vice President of the U.S.

Q: Which political party decided to start giving annuity payments to immigrants?

AND MY FAVORITE:

A: That's right! Jimmy Carter and the Democratic Party.

Immigrants moved into this country, and at age 65, they began to receive Social Security payments! The Democratic Party gave these payments to them even though they never paid a dime into it!

Then, after violating the original contract (FICA), the Democrats turn around and tell you that the Republicans want to take your Social Security away! And the worst part about it is uninformed citizens believe it!

If enough people receive this, maybe a seed of awareness will be planted and maybe changes will evolve. Maybe not, some Democrats are awfully sure of what isn't so.

But it's worth a try. How many people can you send this to? Actions speak louder than bumper stickers. And Congress gives themselves 100% retirement for only serving one term!!!

'A government big enough to give you everything you want, is strong enough to take everything you have.'

-Thomas Jefferson

OBAMA'S OWN WORDS. .THINK ABOUT THIS

PLEASE READ THE LAST LINE!!

Subject: In Obama's own words

This guy wants to be our President and control our government. Pay close attention to the last comment!! Below are a few lines from Obama's books using his words:

From DREAMS OF MY FATHER: 'I ceased to advertise my mother's race at the age of 12 or 13, when I began to suspect that by doing so I was ingratiating myself to whites.'

From DREAMS OF MY FATHER: 'I found a solace in nursing a pervasive sense of grievance and animosity against my mother's race.'

From DREAMS OF MY FATHER: 'There was something about him that made me wary, a little too sure of himself, maybe. And white.'

From DREAMS OF MY FATHER: 'It remained necessary to prove which side you were on, to show your loyalty to the black masses, to strike out and name names.'

From DREAMS OF MY FATHER: 'I never emulate white men and brown men whose fates didn't speak to my own. It was into my father's image, the black man, son of Africa , that I'd packed all the attributes I sought in myself, the attributes of Martin and Malcolm, Dubois and Mandela.'

From AUDACITY OF HOPE: 'I will stand with the Muslims should the political winds shift in an ugly direction.'
If you ever forwarded an e-mail, now is the time to do it again

---

UN VOTING RECORD

Source: http://www.snopes.com/inboxer/outrage/unvote.asp
Below are the actual voting records of various Arabic/Islamic States which are recorded in both the US State Department and United Nations records:
Kuwait votes against the United States 67% of the time
Qatar votes against the United States 67% of the time
Morocco votes against the United States 70% of the time
United Arab Emirates votes against the U. S. 70% of the time
Jordan votes against the United States 71% of the time
Tunisia votes against the United States 71% of the time
Saudi Arabia votes against the   United States 73% of the time
Yemen votes against the United States 74% of the time
Algeria votes against the United States 74% of the time
Oman votes against the United States 74% of the time
Sudan votes against the United States 75% of the time
Pakistan votes against the United States 75% of the time
Libya votes against the United States 76% of the time
Egypt votes against the   United States 79% of the time
Lebanon votes against the United States 80% of the time
India votes against the United States 81% of the time
Syria votes against the United States 84% of the time
Mauritania votes against the United States 87% of the time

U S Foreign Aid to those that hate us:

Egypt, after voting 79% of the time against the United States, still receives $2 billion annually in US Foreign Aid

Jordan votes 71% against the United States and receives $192,814,000 annually in US Foreign Aid

Pakistan votes 75% against the United States Receives $6,721,000 annually in US Foreign Aid

India votes 81% against the United States Receives $143,699,000 annually

Perhaps it is time to get out of the UN and give the tax savings back to the American workers who have to skimp and sacrifice to pay the taxes (and gasoline). Pass this along to every taxpaying citizen you know...Disgusting isn't it?

NO SENSE

Someone needs to help me understand this. If you do, in fact, agree with it, please delete me from all future contact due to the fact that you are senseless and most definitely a Liberal idiot for whom I want nothing to do with...and please, please take that personal!!

I think the vast differences in compensation between victims of the September 11 attack and those who die serving our country in Uniform are profound. No one is really talking about it either, because you just don't criticize anything having to do with September 11. Well, I can't let the numbers pass by because it says something really disturbing about the entitlement mentality of this country.

If you lost a family member in the September 11 attack, you're going to receive an average of $1,185,000. The range is a minimum guarantee of $250,000, all the way up to $4.7 million.

Now, if you are a surviving family member of an American soldier killed in action, the first check you get is a $6,000 direct death benefit, half of which is taxable. Next, you get $1,750 for burial costs. If you are the surviving spouse, you get $833 a month until you remarry. And there's a payment of $211 per month for each child under 18. When the child hits 18, those payments come to a screeching halt.

Keep in mind that some of the people who are getting an average of $1.185 million up to $4.7 million are complaining that it's not enough. Their deaths were tragic indeed, but for most, they were simply in the wrong place at the wrong time. Soldiers put themselves in harm's way for all of us, and they and their families know the dangers.

We have also learned that some of the victims from the Oklahoma City bombing in 1995 have started an organization asking for the same deal that the September 11 families are getting. In addition to that, some of the families of those bombed in US embassies around the world are now asking for compensation as well.

You see where this is going, don't you? This is part and parcel of over 50-years of entitlement politics in this country. It's just really sad. Every time a pay raise comes up for the military, they usually receive next to nothing of a raise. Now the green machine is in combat in the Middle East while their families have to survive on food stamps and live in low-rent housing. How does this make sense?

However, our own US Congress voted themselves a raise. Many of you don't know that they only have to be in Congress for one-term to receive a pension that is more than $15,000 per month. And most are now equal to being millionaires plus. If some of the military people stay in for 20 years and get out as an E-7, they may receive a pension of $1,000 per month, and the very people who placed them in harm's way receive a pension of $15,000 per month. Wow!!

I would like to see our elected officials pick up a weapon and join ranks before they start cutting out benefits and lowering pay for our sons and daughters who are now fighting.

When do we finally do something about this?' If this doesn't seem fair to you, it is time to forward this to as many people as you can.

How many people CAN YOU send this to?

How many people WILL YOU send this to?

…Again, if you agree with this, DO NOT send it back to me!! I will have absolute disgust for you!!

MORE PELOSI

Scary...

Democratic Logic

And now she is Speaker of the House!!!!!!!!!! Obviously, this woman has a very limited knowledge of economics! She is just as scary as Hillary.

Published: October 22, 2006:

Nancy Pelosi condemned the new record highs of the stock market as "just another example of Bush policies helping the rich get richer." "First Bush cut taxes for the rich and the economy has rebounded with new record low unemployment rates, which only means wealthy employers are getting even wealthier at the expense of the underpaid working class."

She went on to say "Despite the billions of dollars being spent in Iraq our economy is still strong and government tax revenues are at all time highs."What this really means is" that business is exploiting the war effort and working Americans, just to put money in their own pockets."

When questioned about recent stock market highs she responded "Only the rich benefit from these record highs. Working Americans, welfare recipients, the unemployed and minorities are not sharing in these obscene record highs."

"There is no question these windfall profits and income created by the Bush administration need to be taxed at 100% rate and those dollars redistributed to the poor and working class."

"Profits from the stock market do not reward the hard work of our working class who, by their hard work, are responsible for generating these corporate profits that create stock market profits for the rich. We in Congress will need to address this issue to either tax the profits or to control the stock market to prevent this unearned income to flow to the rich."

When asked about the fact that over 80% of all Americans have investments in mutual funds, retirement funds, 401K's, and the stock market she replied "That may be true, but probably only 5% account for 90% of all these investment dollars. That's just more "trickle down" economics claiming that if a corporation is successful that everyone from the CEO to the floor sweeper benefit from higher wages and job security which is ridiculous." How much of this "trickle down" ever get to the unemployed and minorities in our county? None, and that's the tragedy of these stock market highs." "We Democrats are going to address this issue after the election when we take control of the Congress. We will return to the 60% to 80% tax rates on the rich and we will be able to take at least 30% of all current lower Federal Income Tax taxpayers off the roles and increase government income substantially. We need to work toward the goal of equalizing income in our country and at the same time limiting the amount the rich can invest."

When asked how these new tax dollars would be spent, she replied "We need to raise the standard of living of our poor, unemployed and minorities. For example, we have an estimated 12 million illegal immigrants in our country who need our help along with millions of unemployed minorities. Stock market windfall profits taxes could go a long ways to guarantee these people the standard of living they would like to have as "Americans."

WORSE THAN YOU THOUGHT & WORTH REMEMBERING

This came from a Democrat

Dear Mr. Ex President Clinton,

I recently saw a bumper sticker that said, "Thank me, I voted for Clinton-Gore." So, I sat down and reflected on that, and I am sending my "Thank you" for what you have done, specifically:

1) Thank you for introducing us to Jennifer Flowers, Paula Jones, Monica Lewinsky, Dolly Kyle Browning, Kathleen Willey, and Juanita Broderick. Did I leave anyone out?

2) Thank you for teaching my 8 year old about oral sex. I had really planned to wait until he was a little older to discuss it with him, but now he knows more about it than I did as a senior in college.

3) Thank you for showing us that sexual harassment in the work place (especially the White House) and on the job is OK, and all you have to know is what the meaning of "it" is. It really is great to know that certain sexual acts are not sex, and one person may have sex while the other one does not have sex

4) Thank you for reintroducing the concept of impeachment to a new generation and demonstrating that the ridiculous plot of the movie "Wag the Dog" could be plausible after all.

5) Thanks for making Jimmy Carter look competent, Gerald Ford look graceful, Richard Nixon look honest, Lyndon Johnson look truthful, and John Kennedy look moral.

6) Thank you for the 73 House and Senate witnesses who have pled the 5th Amendment and 17 witnesses who have fled the country to avoid testifying about Democratic campaign fund raising.

7) Thank you, for the 19 charges, 8 convictions, and 4 imprisonment's from the Whitewater "mess" and the 55 criminal charges and 32 criminal convictions (so far) in the other "Clinton " scandals.

8) Thanks also for reducing our military by half, "gutting" much of our foreign policy, and flying all over the world on "vacations" carefully disguised as necessary trips.

9) Thank you, also, for "finding" millions of dollars (I really didn't need it in the first place, and I can't think of a more deserving group of recipients for my hard-earned tax dollars) for all of your

globe-trotting. I understand you, the family and your cronies have logged in more time aboard Air Force One than any other administration.

10) Now that you've left the White House, thanks for the 140 pardons of convicted felons and indicted felons-in-exile. We will love to have them rejoin society (Not to mention the scores you pardoned while Governor of Arkansas)

11) Thanks also for removing the White House silverware. I'm sure that Laura Bush didn't like the pattern anyway. Also, enjoy the housewarming gifts you've received from your "friends."

12) Thanks to you and your staff in the West Wing of the White House for vandalizing and destroying government property on the way out. I also appreciate removing all of that excess weight (China, silverware, linen, towels, ash trays, soap, pens, magnetic compass, flight manuals, etc.) out of Air Force 1. The weight savings means burning less fuel, thus less tax dollars spent on jet fuel. Thank you!

13) Please ensure that Hillary enjoys the $8 million dollar advance for her "tell-all" book and you, Bill, the $10 million advance for your memoirs. Who says crime doesn't pay!

14) The last and most important point - thank you for forcing Israel to let Mohammed Atta go free. Terrorist pilot Mohammed Atta blew up a bus in Israel in 1986. The Israelis captured, tried and imprisoned him. As part of the Oslo agreement with the Palestinians in 1993, Israel had to agree to release so-called "political prisoners". However, the Israelis would not release any with blood on their hands. The American President at the

time, Bill Clinton, and his Secretary of State, Warren Christopher, "insisted" that all prisoners be released. Thus Mohammed Atta was freed and eventually thanked the US by flying an airplane into Tower One of the World Trade Center. This was reported by many of the American TV networks at the time that the terrorists were first identified. It was censored in the US from all later reports. Why shouldn't Americans know the real truth?

What a guy!!

If you agree that the American public must be made aware of these facts, pass this on. God bless America and thank you (once again) for spending my taxes so wisely and frugally.

Sincerely,

A US Citizen

PS. Please pass along a special thank you to Al Gore for "inventing" the Internet, without which I would not be able to send this wonderful, factual e-mail.

AND THE REST OF THE STORY

Hillary Rodham Clinton, as a New York State Senator, now comes under the "Congressional Retirement and Staffing Plan,"
which means that even if she never gets reelected, she still receives her Congressional salary until she dies. (Would it not be nice if all Americans were pension eligible after only 4 years?).

If Bill outlives her, he then inherits her salary until he dies. He is already getting his Presidential salary until he dies. If
Hillary outlives Bill, she also gets his salary until she dies. Guess

who pays for that? We do!

It's common knowledge that in order for her to establish NY residency, they purchased a million dollar-plus house in upscale Chappaqua, New York. Makes sense. They are entitled to Secret Service protection for life. Still makes sense.

Here is where it becomes interesting. Their mortgage payments hover at around $10,000 per month. But, an extra residence had to be built within the acreage to house the Secret Service agents.

The Clintons charge the Federal government $10,000 monthly rent for the use of that extra residence, which is just about equal to their mortgage payment. This means that we, the taxpayers, are paying the Clinton's salary, mortgage, transportation, safety and security, as well as the salaries for their 12 man staff -- and, this is all perfectly legal!

When she runs for President, will you vote for her?

How many people can you send this to?

Wake up America!

WAS GEORGE W. BUSH A DUMMY?

And you think George W. Bush was a dummy?

Really? Forget Democrat or Republican for a minute and think about this.

You Obama supporters, be honest now. Read the following and tell me how you would have reacted:

1) If George W. Bush had made a joke at the expense of the Special Olympics, would you have approved?

2) If George W. Bush had given Gordon Brown a set of inexpensive

and incorrectly formatted DVDs, when Gordon Brown had given him a thoughtful and historically significant gift, would you have approved?

3) If George W. Bush had given the Queen of England an iPod containing videos of his speeches, would you have thought this embarrassingly narcissistic and tacky?

4) If George W. Bush had bowed to the King of Saudi Arabia, would you have approved?

5) If George W. Bush had visited Austria and made reference to the non-existent "Austrian language," would you have brushed it off as a minor slip?

6) If George W. Bush had filled his cabinet and circle of advisers with people who cannot seem to keep current on their income taxes, would you have approved?

7) If George W. Bush had been so Spanish illiterate as to refer to "Cinco de Cuatro" in front of the Mexican ambassador when it was the fourth of May (Cuatro de Mayo), and continued to flub it when he tried again, would you have winced in embarrassment?

8) If George W. Bush had miss-spelled the word advice would you have hammered him for it for years like Dan Quayle and potatoe as "proof" of what a dunce he is?

9) If George W. Bush had burned 9,000 gallons of jet fuel to go plant a single tree on "Earth Day", would you have concluded he's a hypocrite?

10) If George W. Bush's administration had okayed Air Force One flying low over millions of people followed by a jet fighter in downtown Manhattan causing widespread panic, would you have

wondered whether they actually "get" what happened on 9-11?

11) If George W. Bush had been the first President to need a teleprompter installed to be able to get through a press conference, would you have laughed and said this is more proof of how inept he is on his own and is really controlled by smarter men behind the scenes?

12) If George W. Bush had failed to send relief aid to flood victims throughout the Midwest with more people killed or made homeless than in New Orleans, would you want it made into a major ongoing political issue with claims of racism and incompetence?

13) If George W. Bush had ordered the firing of the CEO of a major corporation, even though he had no constitutional authority to do so, would you have approved?

14) If George W. Bush had proposed to double the national debt, which had taken more than two centuries to accumulate, in one year, would you have approved?

15) If George W. Bush had then proposed to double the debt again 10 times within years, would you have approved?

16) If George W. Bush had reduced your retirement plan's holdings of GM stock by 90% and given the unions a majority stake in GM, would you have approved?

17) If George W. Bush had spent hundreds of thousands of dollars to take Laura Bush to a play in NYC, would you have approved?

18) If George W. Bush had said that three police officers doing their jobs had "acted stupidly" when questioning a friend of his, thus causing a major national racial incident, would you have

approved?

19) If George W. Bush wanted to release terrorist detainees to federal prisons on U.S. soil, which would house them with military prisoners, would you have approved?

20) So, tell me again, what is it about Obama that makes him so brilliant and impressive? Can't think of anything? Don't worry. He's done all the above in just 6 months -- so be patient you've still got three years and six months to come up with an answer.

A NEW DIRECTION FOR AMERICA - LET'S REVIEW THE FACTS

Campaign slogan:

"A New Direction For America -- Vote Democratic!"*

Let's analyze this empty and misleading promise.

1) The stock market is at a new all-time high and America's 401K's are back. A new direction from there means what?

2) Unemployment is at 25 year lows. A new direction from there means what?

3) Oil prices are plummeting. A new direction from there means what?

4) Taxes are at 20 year lows. A new direction from there means what?

5) Federal tax revenues are at all-time highs. A new direction from there means what?

6) The Federal deficit is down almost 50%, just as predicted over last year. A new direction from there means what?

7) Home valuations are up 200% over the past 3.5 years. A new direction from there means what?

8) Inflation is in check, hovering at 20 year lows. A new direction from there means what?

9) Not a single terrorist attack on US soil since 9/11/01. A new direction from there means what?

10) Osama bin Laden is living under a rock in a dark cave, having not surfaced in years, if he's alive at all, while 95% of Al Queda's top dogs are either dead or in custody, cooperating with US Intel. A new direction from there means what?

11) Several major terrorist attacks already thwarted by US and British Intel, including the recent planned attack involving 10 Jumbo Jets being exploded in mid-air over major US cities in order to celebrate the anniversary of the 9/11/01 attacks A new direction from there means what?

12) Just as Bush had planned and foretold us on a number of occasions, Iraq was to be made "ground zero" for the war on terrorism -- and just as Bush said they would, terrorist cells from all over the region are alighting the shadows of their hiding places and flooding into Iraq in order to get their faces blown off by US Marines rather than boarding planes and heading to the United States to wage war on us here. A new direction from there means what?

Moreover, bear in mind that all of the above occurred in the face of the 1999 tech crash, the epidemic of corporate scandals throughout the 90's, and the 9/11/01 terrorist attacks on NYC years in the planning which collectively sucked 24 trillion dollars and 7.8 million jobs out of the US economy even before G. W. Bush had time to unpack his suitcases in the White House.

It's easy for the Democrats to attempt to discredit, disgrace and defame our commander in chief, George W. Bush -- that's what they do. What's not so easy for them to do is to refute irrefutable facts, no matter how they might try.

Do yourself and this country of ours a favor and don't be a mindless sheep or a blind Liberal lap dog, bent on hate and blame-shifting simply in the name of hate and blame-shifting. Take heed of reality, use your head and cast your vote wisely in the upcoming elections. The stakes are far too high today, as America's very future, and yes, even its very survival is now at stake.

LET'S SAY I BREAK INTO YOUR HOUSE...

Recently large demonstrations have taken place across the country protesting the fact that Congress is finally addressing the issue of illegal immigration. Certain people are angry that the US might protect its own borders, might make it harder to sneak into this country and, once here, to stay indefinitely. Let me see if I correctly understand the thinking behind these protests.

Let's say I break into your house. Let's say that when you discover me in your house, you insist that I leave. But I say, "I've made all the beds and washed the dishes and did the laundry and swept the floors; I've done all the things you don't like to do. I'm hard-working and honest(except for when I broke into your house).

According to the protesters, not only must you let me stay, you must add me to your family's insurance plan, educate my kids, and provide other benefits to me and to my family (my husband will do your yard work because he too is hard-working and honest, except for that breaking in part).

If you try to call the police or force me out, I will call my friends who will picket your house carrying signs that proclaim my right to be there. It's only fair, after all, because you have a nicer house than I do, and I'm just trying to better myself. I'm hard-working and honest, um, except for well, you know.

And what a deal it is for me!! I live in your house, contributing only a fraction of the cost of my keep, and there is nothing you can do about it without being accused of selfishness, prejudice and being an anti-housebreaker. Oh yeah, and I want you to learn my language so you can communicate with me.

Why can't people see how ridiculous this is?! Only in America ....if you agree, pass it on (in English). Share it if you see the value of it as a good simile. If not blow it off along with your future Social Security funds.

A TRUISM

A woman in a hot air balloon realized she was lost. She lowered altitude and spotted a man in a boat below. She shouted to him," excuse me, can you help me? I promised a friend I would meet him an hour ago, but I don't know where I am!"

The man consulted his portable GPS and replied, "You're in a hot air balloon approximately 39 feet above sea level. You're 31 degrees, 14.97 minutes north latitude and 100 degrees, 49.09 minutes west longitude.

She rolled her eyes and said, "You must be a Republican."

"I am" replied the man. "How did you guess?"

"Well," she said, "everything you said was technically correct, but I have no idea what to make of your information, and I'm still lost. Frankly, you've not been much help to me."

The man smiled and answered,"! You must be a Democrat."

"I am," she said, "how did you know?"

"Well" said the man, "you don't know where you are, or where you're going, you've risen to where you are, due to a quantity of hot air, you've made a promise that you have no idea how to keep, and you expect me to solve your problem. You're in exactly the same position you were in before we met, but somehow, now it's all my fault!"

THIS IS HOW THE MEDIA PERCEIVES THINGS!

Subject: Pope visits Bush

The Pope is visiting Washington, D.C., and President Bush takes him out for an afternoon on the Potomac, cruising on the Presidential yacht, the Sequoia. They're admiring the sights when, all of a sudden, the Pope's hat (zucchetto) blows off his head and out into the water.

Secret Service guys start to launch a boat, but President Bush waves them off, saying, "Wait, wait. I'll take care of this. Don't worry."

Bush then steps off the yacht onto the   surface of the water and walks out to the Holy Father's little hat, bends over, picks it up, and then walks back to the yacht and climbs aboard. He hands the hat to the Pope amid stunned silence.

The next morning, the headlines in the New York Times, Boston Globe, Atlanta Constitution, Washington Post, Boston Herald,

Buffalo News, Houston Chronicle, Milwaukee Sentinel-Journal, Minneapolis Tribune, Denver Post, Albuquerque Journal, Los Angeles Times, and San Francisco Chronicle all proclaim: "Bush Can't Swim!"

UNBELIEVABLE

This is old. I have never even seen one...thank God!! A few names have been changed. Why would they make this stamp .42 cents and then you have to purchase a .03 cent stamp just for the postal service to pick up. To mail a letter in the US cost $0.44 today. You can believe if this stamp does exist, I will not purchase it...and if I ever receive any mail with this stamp on it...I will refuse it and in big letters write on it:

Return to sender...an American lives here...!!!

This is really scary!!

Read the very last comment...how true it is

USPS 42-Cent Stamp!!! Celebrates Muslim holiday.

If there is only ONE thing you forward today, let it be this!

Remember the Muslim bombing of Pan Am flight 103!

Remember the Muslim bombing of the world trade center in 1993!

Remember the Muslim bombing of the marine barracks in Lebanon!

Remember the Muslim bombing of the military barracks in Saudi Arabia!

Remember the Muslim bombing of the American embassies in Africa!

Remember the Muslim bombing of the USS Cole!

Remember the Muslim attack on 9/11/2001!

Remember all the American lives that were lost in those vicious Muslim attacks!

Now President Obama has directed the United States Postal Service to remember and honor the EID MUSLIM holiday season with a commemorative 42-Cent First Class Holiday Postage Stamp.

Remember to adamantly & vocally boycott this stamp, when you are purchasing your stamps at the post office.

All you have to say is "No thank you, I do not want that Muslim Stamp on my letters!"

To use this stamp would be a slap in the face to all those Americans who died at the hands of those whom this stamp honors.

Remember:

Pass this along to every patriotic American that you know and let's get the word out!!!

Here is something to chew on...

They (Muslims) don't even believe in Christ, & they're getting their own Christmas stamp! And Christians can no longer say a prayer in public schools...or have a bible or the Ten Commandments placed on federal, state or city property...and they want to call me a racist!!!!
This is truly unbelievable!!

RACISM

Obama says we need to have a conversation about race in America. Fair enough. But this time, it has to be a two-way conversation. White America needs to be heard from, not just lectured to... This time, the silent majority needs to have its convictions, grievances and demands heard. And among them are these:

First, America has been the best country on earth for black folks. It was here that 600,000 black people, brought from Africa in slave ships, grew into a community of 40 million, were introduced to Christian salvation, and reached the greatest levels of freedom and prosperity blacks have ever known. Rev. Wright ought to go down on his knees and thank God he is an American.

SECOND, no people anywhere has done more to lift up blacks than white Americans. Untold trillions have been spent since the '60s on welfare, food stamps, rent supplements, Section 8 housing, Pell grants, student loans, legal services, Medicaid, Earned Income Tax Credits and poverty programs designed to bring the African-American community into the mainstream. Governments, businesses and colleges have engaged in discrimination against white folks -- with affirmative action, contract set-asides and quotas -- to advance black applicants over white applicants. Churches, foundations, civic groups, schools and individuals all over America have donated their time and money to support soup kitchens, adult education, day care, retirement and nursing homes for blacks.

We hear the grievances.

Where is the gratitude??

Obama talks about new 'ladders of opportunity' for blacks. Let him go to Altoona? And Johnstown , and ask the white kids in Catholic schools how many were visited lately by Ivy League recruiters handing out scholarships for 'deserving' white kids? Is white America really responsible for the fact that the crime and incarceration rates for African-Americans are seven times those of white America? Is it really white America's fault that illegitimacy in the African-American community has hit 70 percent and the black dropout rate from high schools in some cities has reached 50 percent?

Is that the fault of white America or, first and foremost, a failure of the black community itself?

As for racism, its ugliest manifestation is in interracial crime, and especially interracial crimes of violence. Is Obama aware that while white criminals choose black victims 3 percent of the time, black criminals choose white victims 45 percent of the time?

Is Obama aware that black-on-white rapes are 100 times more common than the reverse; that black-on-white robberies were 139 times as common in the first three years of this decade as the reverse?

We have all heard ad nauseam from the Rev. Al about Tawana Brawley, the Duke rape case and Jena. And all turned out to be hoaxes. But about the epidemic of black assaults on whites that are real, we hear nothing.

Sorry, Obama, some of us have heard it all before, about 40 years and 40 trillion tax dollars ago.

We are a Christian Nation Even if Obama says we are not...

HEALTH CARE

Let me get this straight.

We're going to pass a health care plan written by a committee whose head says he doesn't understand it, passed by a Congress that hasn't read it but exempts themselves from it, signed by a president that also hasn't read it, and who smokes, with funding administered by a treasury chief who didn't pay his taxes, overseen by a surgeon general who is obese, and financed by a country that's nearly broke. What possibly could go wrong?

WELCOME TO OUR CHANGE

Subject: Plumbing Problems at Obama's Home

Obama discovers a leak under his sink, so he calls Joe the Plumber to come and fix it. Joe drives to Obama's house, which is located in a very nice neighborhood and where it's clear that all the residents make more than $250,000 per year.

Joe arrives and takes his tools into the house. Joe is led to the room that contains the leaky pipe under a sink. Joe assesses the problem and tells Obama, who is standing near the door, that it's an easy repair that will take less than 10 minutes. Obama asks Joe how much it will cost. Joe immediately says, '$9,500.'

'$9,500?' Obama asks, stunned. 'But you said it's an easy repair!'

'Yes, but what I do is charge a lot more to my clients who make more than $250,000 per year so I can fix the plumbing of everybody who makes less than that for free,' explains Joe. 'It's always been my philosophy. As a matter of fact, I lobbied government to pass this philosophy as law, and it did pass earlier this year, so now all plumbers have to do business this way. It's known as 'Joe's Fair Plumbing Act of 2008.' Surprised you haven't heard of it, senator.'

In spite of that, Obama tells Joe there's no way he's paying that much for a small plumbing repair, so Joe leaves. Obama spends the next hour flipping through the phone book looking for another plumber, but he finds that all other plumbing businesses listed have gone out of business. Not wanting to pay Joe's price, Obama does nothing. The leak under Obama's sink goes unrepaired for the next several days. A week later the leak is so bad that Obama has had to put a bucket under the sink. The bucket fills up quickly and has to be emptied every hour, and there's a risk that the room will flood, so Obama calls Joe and pleads with him to return.

Joe goes back to Obama's house, looks at the leaky pipe, and says 'Let's see - this will cost you about $21,000.

'A few days ago you told me it would cost $9,500!' Obama quickly fires back. Joe explains the reason for the dramatic increase.

'Well, because of the 'Joe's Fair Plumbing Act,' a lot of rich people are learning how to fix their own plumbing, so there are fewer of you paying for all the free plumbing I'm doing for the people who make less than $250,000. As a result, the rate I have to charge my wealthy paying customers rises every day. Not only that, but for some reason the demand for plumbing work from the group of people who get it for free has skyrocketed, and there's a long waiting list of those who need repairs. This has put a lot of my fellow plumbers out of business, and they're not being replaced - nobody is going into the plumbing business because they know they won't make any money. I'm hurting now too - all thanks to greedy rich people like you who won't pay their fair share.'

Obama tries to straighten out the plumber: 'Of course you're hurting, Joe! Don't you get it? If all the rich people learn how to fix their own plumbing and you refuse to charge the poorer people for your services, you'll be broke, and then what will you do?'

Joe immediately replies, 'Run for president, apparently.'

GENERAL EISENHOWER WARNED US

It is a matter of history that when the Supreme Commander of the Allied Forces, General Dwight Eisenhower, found the victims of the death camps he ordered all possible photographs to be taken, and for the German people from surrounding villages to be ushered through the camps and even made to bury the dead.

He did this because he said in words to this effect:

'Get it all on record now - get the films - get the witnesses -because somewhere down the road of history some bastard will get up and say that this never happened.

This week, the UK debated whether to remove The Holocaust from its school curriculum because it 'offends' the Muslim population which claims it never occurred. It is not removed as yet. However, this is a frightening portent of the fear that is gripping the world and how easily each country is giving into it.

It is now more than 60 years after the Second World War in Europe ended. This e-mail is being sent as a memorial chain, in memory of the, 6 million Jews, 20 million Russians, 10 million Christians, and 1,900 Catholic priests who were murdered, raped, burned, starved, beat, experimented on and humiliated' while the German people looked the other way!

Now, more than ever, with Iran , among others, claiming the Holocaust to be 'a myth,' it is imperative to make sure the world never forgets.

This e-mail is intended to reach 400 million people! Be a link in the memorial chain and help distribute this around the world.

How many years will it be before the attack on the World Trade Center 'never happened'? Because it offends some Muslim in the U.S.???

Freedom isn't free...someone had to pay for it

If you can read this ... thank a teacher

If you can read this in English ... thank a veteran

God Bless America!

THE ECONOMIC MESS

Dear Friends, .

I am sounding an alarm! For the life of me, I cannot figure out why this is not being discussed on the media or why Conservatives are not making their case: It is so important!!!!! The following is a condensation of a series from the Investor's Business Daily explaining "What Caused the Loan Crisis":

1977: Pres. Jimmy Carter signs the Community Reinvestment Act into Law. The law pressured financial institutions to extend home loans to those who would otherwise not qualify. The Premise: Home ownership would improve poor and crime-ridden communities and neighborhoods in terms of crime, investment, jobs, etc.

Results: Statistics bear out that it did not help.

How did the government get so deeply involved in the housing market?

Answer: Bill Clinton wanted it that way.

1992: Republican representative Jim Leach (IO) warned of the danger that Fannie and Freddie were changing from being agencies of the public at large to money machines for the principals and the stockholding few.

1993: Clinton extensively rewrote Fannie Mae and Freddie Mac's rules turning the quasi-private mortgage-funding firms into semi-nationalized monopolies dispensing cash and loans to large Democratic voting blocks and handing favors, jobs and contributions to political allies. This potent mix led inevitably to corruption and now the collapse of Freddie and Fannie.

1994: Despite warnings, Clinton unveiled his National Home-Ownership Strategy which broadened the CRA in ways Congress never intended.

1995: Congress, about to change from a Democrat majority to Republican, Clinton orders Robert Rubin's Treasury Dept to rewrite the rules. Robert. Rubin's Treasury reworked rules, forcing banks to satisfy quotas for sub-prime and minority loans to get a satisfactory CRA rating. The rating was key to expansion or mergers for banks. Loans began to be made on the basis of race and little else.

1997 - 1999: Clinton, bypassing Republicans, enlisted Andrew Cuomo, then Secretary of Housing and Urban Development, allowing Freddie and Fannie to get into the sub-prime market in a big way. Led by Rep. Barney Frank and Sen. Chris Dodd, Congress doubled down on the risk by easing capital limits and allowing them to hold just 2.5% of capital to back their investments vs. 10% for banks. Since they could borrow at lower rates than banks their enterprises boomed.

With incentives in place, banks poured billions in loans into poor communities, often "no doc", "no income", requiring no money down and no verification of income.   Worse still was the cronyism: Fannie and Freddie became home to out-of work-politicians, mostly Clinton Democrats. 384 politicians got big campaign donations from Fannie and Freddie. Over $200 million had been spent on lobbying and political activities. During the 1990's Fannie and Freddie enjoyed a subsidy of as much as $182-billion, most of it going to principals and shareholders, not poor borrowers as claimed. Did it work? Minorities made up 49% of the 12.5 million new homeowners but many of those loans have gone bad and the minority homeownership rates are shrinking fast.

1999: New Treasury Secretary, Lawrence Summers, became alarmed at Fannie and Freddie's excesses. Congress held hearings the ensuing year but nothing was done because Fannie and Freddie had donated millions to key Congressmen and radical groups, ensuring no meaningful changes would take place. "We manage our political risk with the same intensity that we manage our credit and interest rate risks," Fannie CEO Franklin Raines, a former Clinton official and current Obama advisor, bragged to investors in 1999.

2000: Secretary Summers sent Undersecretary Gary Gensler to Congress seeking an end to the "special status". Democrats raised a ruckus as did Fannie and Freddie, headed by politically connected CEO's who knew how to reward and punish. "We think that the statements evidence a contempt for the nation's housing and mortgage markets" Freddie spokesperson Sharon McHale said. It was the last chance during the Clinton era for reform.

2001: Republicans try repeatedly to bring fiscal sanity to Fannie and Freddie but Democrats blocked any attempt at reform; especially Rep. Barney Frank and Sen. Chris Dodd who now run key banking committees and were huge beneficiaries of campaign contributions from the mortgage giants.

2003: Bush proposes what the NY Times called "the most significant regulatory overhaul in the housing finance industry since the savings and loan crisis a decade ago". Even after discovering a scheme by Fannie and Freddie to overstate earnings by $10.6 billion to boost their bonuses, the Democrats killed reform.

2005: Then Fed chairman Alan Greenspan warns Congress: "We are placing the total financial system at substantial risk". Sen. McCain, with two others, sponsored a Fannie/Freddie reform bill and said, "If Congress does not act, American taxpayers will continue to be exposed to the enormous risk that Fannie Mae and Freddie Mac pose to the housing market, the overall financial system and the economy as a whole". Sen. Harry Reid accused the GOP; of trying to "cripple the ability of Fannie and Freddie to carry out their mission of expanding homeownership" The bill went nowhere.

2007: By now Fannie and Freddie own or guarantee over half of the $12-trillion U.S. mortgage market. The mortgage giants, whose executive suites were top-heavy with former Democratic officials, had been working with Wall St. to repackage the bad loans and sell them to investors. As the housing market fell in '07, subprime mortgage portfolios suffered major losses. The crisis was on, though it was 15 years in the making.

2008: McCain has repeatedly called for reforming the behemoths, Bush urged reform 17 times. Still the media have repeated Democrats' talking points about this being a "Republican" disaster. A few Republicans are complicit but Fannie and Freddie were created by Democrats, regulated by Democrats, largely run by Democrats and protected by Democrats. That's why taxpayers are now being asked for $700 billion!!

If you doubt any of this, just click the links below and listen to your lawmakers own words. They are condemning!

http://www.youtube.com/watch?v=68D9XrqyrWo&feature=related#

http://www.youtube.com/watch?v=pIgqfM5C8lY#

http://www.youtube.com/watch?v=H9juJr8CSY4&feature=related#

Postscript: ACORN is one of the principle beneficiaries of Fannie/Freddie's slush funds. They are currently under indictment or investigation in many states. Obama served as their legal counsel, defending their activities for several years.

Please share this with everyone you know. Send it. Print it. Talk about it. America needs to know!!!

CYNICAL ALASKAN

How Sarah Palin Handled Corruption

From an Alaskan who is a very serious cynic about all things political, here is my take on Sarah.

I met and spoke with Sarah Palin about two years ago at our downtown park strip. It is a place for walking, carnivals, political outdoor things and such. She was cooking hotdogs at a fund raiser and introducing herself to the public as a Governor hopeful.

She came by and said the usual "Hi, I'm Sarah Palin and I am running for Governor"...and I expected her to keep on to the next person but she asked me who I was and what I did in Alaska and we ended up talking for 15 minutes about me, Air America (she was all agog!) and my career in the Army and AAM. She is a pilot (Super Cub) I'm told, although all she told me about that was that she loved flying.

As I watched her successful run for governor over the next six months, I was really impressed. In fact I already was impressed greatly even before that, after she resigned a good position (Alaska Gas and Oil Regulatory Commission) because a fellow Commission member (Chair of the Alaska Republican Party) misused his office and position. He was using the fax, computers, printing room and all to promote the Republican endeavors while in a state job. That is a huge no-no in any government employment position.

She resigned and made her point, and within weeks Randy Ruderich (the above bad guy) found his butt out on the street and a subsequent investigation found him guilty and he was fined $12,000. Small change actually but a giant point was made.

Next she went after our most horrible Governor ever, Governor Murkowski, and damned if she didn't beat him! All of us here in Alaska, except the Democrats, are sick of our state's corruption. That fact was shouted to the heavens after she was elected with an overwhelming point spread.

After she got into office she started going after corrupt legislators, and with the FBI's help we've put four of them in prison, indicted six more and the "Corrupt Bastard's Club" as they arrogantly called themselves (even had hats made with CBC on the front!) suddenly found it no fun anymore.

The current flap which has cost her a ten point loss of popularity (She's still 82 %!) was over firing a popular Commissioner of Public Safety who is responsible for our Alaska State Troopers. She fired him for no stated reason, which was her prerogative as the governor. He served entirely at her option. She and her whole family had a bad, bad experience with a rogue Trooper who was married to Sarah's sister. His name is Trooper Wooten. This dimwit Trooper had threatened Sarah's father (death threat!), threatened Sarah ("I'll get you too"), Tasered his 12 year old stepson, drove drunk in his AST cruiser, got a pass by a fellow Trooper who stopped him for erratic driving a second time while in civvies, and just a host of other things not yet released to the public. He got away with it and got another pass by the Commissioner's appointed AST Trooper Internal Affairs investigator with a tiny slap on the wrist. Five days off without pay to be exact.

This maverick Trooper is still on the payroll but only just. The union's intervention saved his malcontent butt. He'll yet get his, I'm sure. Incredible heat is being heaped on the Troopers. Public heat, not the Governor's office.

The Democrats had the audacity to appoint an obviously biased investigator, Rep. "Gunny" French (so called because he lied about being in the USMC while running for the legislature) is a staunch Liberal and probably under the orders of Senate President Lyda Green who hates Sarah. She hates Sarah because after being elected Governor Sarah told the whole Legislature in one of her first meetings with them that, quote; "All of you here need some Adult Supervision!"

Sarah was seriously angry and not afraid of anyone there. That played wonderfully well with Alaskans. The whole legislature was angry back at her and still are, but also afraid of her because of her popularity.

She reminds me personally of our Alaska wolverine which will fight anything in its path if it sees fit to do so. No respect at all for size or position.

In closing I must tell you that she is the best, most moral and most focused leader I've seen since President Reagan. I feel, really strongly that like Alaska, the rest of our country will love her within a few weeks. Put simply, she represents Middle America like no leader we've ever had.

I think McCain made a totally brilliant move in choosing her. She's a maverick who is probably tougher and more focused than McCain himself... and she won't be a total yes man, or more appropriately, yes woman.

McCain will love her.

In 2012 she will be President.

THE COLONEL AND LINCOLN... POWERFUL

Take a few moments and read this letter. These are strong, powerful and courageous words coming from a retired colonel, and read what Lincoln had to say at the end.

Wow. 33 Senators (including Obama) voted against English as America's Official Language on June 6, 2007

The colonel USA, Ret. wrote:

Senators:

Your vote against an amendment to the immigration Bill 1348... To make English America's official language is astounding.

On D-Day, no less, when we honor those that sacrificed in order to secure the bedrock, character and principles of America, I can only surmise your vote reflects a loyalty to illegal aliens.

I don't much care where you come from. What your religion is. Whether you're black, white, or some other color...male or female......Democrat, Republican or Independent....... But I do care when you are a United States Senator representing Citizens of America ...and Vote against English as the official language of the United States.

Your vote reflects betrayal, political surrender and violates your Pledge of Allegiance. It dishonors historical principle, rejects Patriotism, borders on traitorous action and, in my opinion, makes you unfit to serve as a United States Senator. Impeachment, recall, or other appropriate action is warranted, or worse.

Four of you, voting against English as America's Official Language are current Presidential Candidates: Senator Biden, Senator Clinton, Senator Dodd and Senator Obama.

Four Senators vying to lead America, but won't, or don't, have the courage to cast a vote in favor of English as America's Official Language when 91% of American Citizens want English officially designated as our language.

This is the second time in the last several months this list of Senators have disgraced themselves as 'political Hacks'..... Unworthy as Senators and certainly unqualified to serve as President of the United States.

If America is as angry as I am, you will realize a backlash so stunning it will literally 'rock you out of your socks' and, preferably, totally out of the United States Senate.

The entire immigration bill is a farce...Your action only confirms this really isn't about America... it is about self-serving politics, despicable at best. It has been said: 'Never argue with an Idiot....They'll drag you down to their level!

And now, Mr. Lincoln, selectively-remembered for some things that are now so easily forgotten...

President Abraham Lincoln said: 'Congressmen, who willfully take actions during wartime that damages morale and undermines the military, are saboteurs and should be arrested, quickly tried and hanged!!!

Please keep this going around the United States until the election in November!

GIRD YOURSELF FOR FURTHER TAX PAIN

There have been several articles since the 'anointed one' made his tax plan public last week. None of the effects bode well for anyone on this list. Look at this one. Relative to the article I sent a few weeks back, this would put the tax burden of the top 50% of earners in the US at GREATER that 100%.

Obama's Tax Plan Is Really a Welfare Plan.

Obama's tax plan is the opposite of supply-side economics. He proposes to raise marginal rates for just about every federal tax.

He also proposes a raft of tax credits that taxpayers can receive if they engage in various government-specified activities.

Moreover, the tax credits would mostly go to those who pay little or nothing in federal income taxes. His trick is to make the tax credits "refundable." Thus, if the tax credit is for $1,000, but the taxpayer would otherwise only pay $200 in taxes, the government would write a check to the taxpayer for $800. If the taxpayer pays nothing in federal income taxes, the government would pay him the whole $1,000.

Such credits are not tax cuts. Indeed, they should be called The New Tax Welfare. In effect, Mr. Obama is proposing to create or expand a slew of government spending programs that are disguised as tax credits. The spending on these programs is then subtracted from the total tax burden, in order to make the claim that his tax plan is a net tax cut overall.

On the tax side of the ledger, the details released by his campaign last week confirm what a President Obama has in mind for our most productive citizens. The top individual income tax rate, for example, would be increased by 13%, to 39.6%; the next-highest rate would be raised to 36%. The top rates on capital gains and dividends would rise by a third, to 20%

The Social Security payroll tax would be raised between 16% to 32% for families making over $250,000 a year. This means that the real returns these people get from their lifetime payments into the retirement program will be driven below 0%, according to my own previous research, which was published by the Cato Institute and elsewhere.

Mr. Obama also wants a permanent federal estate tax, with a top rate of 45%; his health-insurance plan includes a new payroll tax on employers; and he also contemplates several increases in the corporate income tax, including a new so-called windfall profits tax on oil companies.

Then there is the spending side of the ledger. Mr. Obama proposes a fully refundable Making Work Pay Tax Credit, which would have the government pay out $500 to each worker and $1,000 to couples -- reminiscent of George McGovern's 1972 election proposal for the government to send a $1,000 check to everyone.

His American Opportunity Tax Credit would provide a $4,000, fully refundable tax credit for college tuition expenses. His Mortgage Interest Tax Credit would provide a 10% credit -- refundable -- to offset mortgage interest payments for lower- and middle-income families. His Health Care Tax Credits, which the campaign says "will ensure that health insurance is available and affordable for all families," include "a new refundable 50 percent health tax credit on employee premiums paid by employers."

Currently existing tax credits would also become spending programs in the Obama tax program. The Savers Credit would be made fully refundable, and would be expanded, according to the campaign, "to match 50% of the first $1,000 of savings for families that earn under $75,000." The Child and Dependent Care Tax Credit would be made refundable and expanded to allow "low-income families to receive up to a 50 percent credit on the first $6,000 of child care expenses." The Earned Income Tax Credit is already refundable. Mr. Obama would expand it to "increase the number of working parents eligible for EITC benefits, increase the benefits available to noncustodial parents who fulfill their child support obligations, increase benefits for families with three or more children, and reduce the EITC marriage penalty, which hurts low-income families." In short, welfare spending is to be increased by paying more money out to low-income income tax filers.

The latest Congressional Budget Office data shows the bottom 40% of income earners already pay no income taxes. Indeed, they receive a net payment from the federal income tax system -- meaning from the taxpayers -- equal to 3.8% of all federal income taxes, because of the refundable tax credits under current law. The middle 20% of income earners, the true middle class, pays 4.4% of federal income taxes.

Overall, the bottom 60% of income earners pays less than 1% of federal income taxes on net. When "tax credits" primarily go to this group in the form of checks from the government (rather than a reduction in their tax burden) it is simply an abuse of the language to call the spending a tax cut.

Consequently, to say, as the campaign does say, that the candidate's tax plan is a tax cut on net -- and that it would limit taxes to 18.2% of GDP -- is grossly misleading. The Obama tax plan would sharply increase real taxes. It also would come nowhere near to paying for the massive increases in federal spending he has proposed, including the spending that is disguised in the form of refundable tax credits. Mr. Ferrara is director of entitlement and budget policy for the Institute for Policy Innovation. He served in President Reagan's White House Office of Policy Development, and as associate deputy attorney general under the President George H.W. Bush.

NOW WE KNOW!

Tell me again why people are falling for this guy???

God Bless our soldiers and keep them safe. Pray for them and thank them every time you see them. Had to pass this on. You know this war touches my heart in several different ways. Please read this!

Hello everyone,

As you know I am not a very political person. I just wanted to pass along that Senator Obama came to Bagram, Afghanistan for about an hour during his visit to 'The War Zone'. I wanted to share with you what happened.

He got off the plane and got into a bullet proof vehicle, got to the area to meet with the Major General who is the commander here at Bagram.

Soldiers were lined up to shake his hand but he blew them off and didn't say a word as he went into the conference room to meet the general. After he finished, vehicles took him and his entourage to the Clamshell (pretty much a big top tent where military personnel can play basketball or work out with weights) so he could take his publicity pictures playing basketball. He again shunned the opportunity to talk to soldiers and thank them for their service.

So really he was just here to make a showing for Americans back home. I think that if you are going to make an effort to come all the way over here you would thank those that are providing the freedom you enjoy.

I swear we got more thanks from NBA Basketball Players and the Dallas Cowboy Cheerleaders than from one of the Senators who wants to be the President of the United States. I just don't understand how anyone would want him to be our Commander-and-Chief. It was almost like he was scared to be around those who secure freedom for him and our great country.

If this is blunt and to the point I am sorry, but I wanted you all to know what kind of caliber of person he really is. What you see in the news is all fake.

AN OBAMINATION

My fellow Americans:

As your future President I want to thank my supporters, for your mindless support of me, despite my complete lack of any legislative achievement, my pastor's relations with Louis Farrakhan and Libyan dictator Moamar Quadafi, or my blatantly leftist voting record while I present myself as some sort of bi-partisan agent of change.

I also like how my supporters claim my youthful drug use and criminal behavior somehow qualifies me for the Presidency after 8 years of claiming Bush's youthful drinking disqualifies him. Your hypocrisy is a beacon of hope shining over a sea of political posing.

I would also like to thank the Kennedy's for coming out in support of me. There's alot of glamor behind the Kennedy name, even though JFK accelerated the Vietnam War, his brother Robert illegally wiretapped Martin Luther King, Jr. and Teddy killed a female employee with whom he was having an extra marital affair. And I'm not going anywhere near the cousins, both literally and figuratively. And I'd like to thank Oprah Winfrey for her support. Her love of meaningless empty platitudes will be the force that propels me to the White House.

Americans should vote for me, not because of my lack of experience or achievement, but because I make people feel good. Voting for me causes some white folk to feel relieved of their imagined, racist guilt. I say things that sound meaningful, but don't really mean anything because Americans are tired of things having meaning. If things have meaning, then that means you have to think about them. Americans are tired of thinking. It's time to shut down the brain, and open up the heart. So when you go to vote, remember don't think, just do it...and do it for me.

Thank You,

Obama Hussein Obama, Jr.

HOW COULD WE KNOW

Did you know that 47 countries' have reestablished their embassies in Iraq?

Did you know that the Iraqi government currently employs 1.2 million Iraqi people?

Did you know that 3100 schools have been renovated, 364 schools are under rehabilitation, 263 new schools are now under construction; and 38 new schools have been completed in Iraq?

Did you know that Iraq's higher educational structure consists of 20 Universities, 46 Institutes or colleges and 4 research centers, all currently operating?

Did you know that 25 Iraq students departed for the United States in January 2005 for the re-established Fulbright program?

Did you know that the Iraqi Navy is operational? They have 5 - 100-foot patrol craft, 34 smaller vessels and a naval infantry regiment.

Did you know that Iraq 's Air Force consists of three operational squadrons, which includes 9 reconnaissance and 3 US C-130 transport aircraft (under Iraqi operational control) which operate day and night, and will soon add 16 UH-1 helicopters and 4 Bell Jet Rangers?

Did you know that Iraq has a counter-terrorist unit and a Commando Battalion?

Did you know that the Iraqi Police Service has over 55,000 fully trained and equipped police officers?

Did you know that there are 5 Police Academies in Iraq that produce over 3,500 new officers every 8 weeks?

Many US Soldiers Volunteer for Extended Duty In Iraqi!

Did you know there are more than 1100 building projects going on in Iraq? They include 364 schools, 67 public clinics, 15 hospitals, 83 railroad stations, 22 oil facilities, 93 water facilities and 69 electrical facilities.

Did you know that 96% of Iraqi children under the age of 5 have received the first 2 series of polio vaccinations?

Did you know that 4.3 million Iraqi children were enrolled in primary school by mid October?

Did you know that there are 1,192,000 cell phone subscribers in Iraq and phone use has gone up 158%?

Did you know that Iraq has an independent media that consists of 75 radio stations, 180 newspapers and 10 television stations?

Did you know that the Baghdad Stock Exchange opened in June of 2004?

Did you know that 2 candidates in the Iraqi presidential election had a televised debate recently?

Of course we didn't know

Why didn't we know?

Because our Liberal media won't tell us!

Instead of reflecting our love for our country, we get photos of flag burning incidents at Abu Ghraib and people throwing snowballs at the presidential motorcades.

Tragically, the lack of accentuating the positive in Iraq serves two purposes: It is intended to undermine the world's perception of the United States thus minimizing consequent support; and it is intended to discourage American citizens.

Above facts are verifiable on the Department of Defense web site.

Did you know?

I didn't know

But I know now...

Pass it on! Give it a Wide Dissemination

BEWARE OF HISTORY!

If a Democrat goes into the White House; we will have more of this type of change, so beware of history!

By the way, poor people have been voting for Democrats for over 100 years and they're still poor! I just don't understand why people seem to forget this...

George Bush has been in office for almost 8 years. The first six the economy was fine, then in 2006 the American public voted in a Democratic Congress.

A little over one year ago:

1) Consumer confidence stood at a 2 1/2 year high

2) Regular gasoline sold for $2.19 a gallon

3) The unemployment rate was 4.5%

Since voting in a Democratic Congress in 2006:

1) Consumer confidence plummeted

2) Gasoline soared to over $4 a gallon

3) Unemployment is up to 5% (a 10% increase)

4) American households have seen $2.3 trillion in equity value evaporate, simply from stock and mutual fund losses

5) Americans have seen their home equity drop by $12 trillion

6) More than 1% of American homes are in foreclosure

America voted for change in 2006, and we got it!

USS LAKE ERIE

Homer Hickam made an interesting comment on TV last week. In case you don't know who he is, Homer was a poor West VA miner's son who worked his way up to being an employee/scientist for NASA. He wrote a book called "Rocket Boy" which was later made into a great movie called "October Sky."

This morning he was interviewed and said this, about the one-shot shoot down of the crippled satellite: "If this country's head was on straight, they would be holding a ticker tape parade for the Crew of the Cruiser, USS Lake Erie..."

"This one rocket firing boosted our National defense 100 fold...N Korea, Iran , China , Russia , all know now that we have a safety net that can accurately stop their incoming missiles even if they are out of the earth's atmosphere."

"Of course, that was the plan all along, and it was a dandy plan. I just hope that the next person in the White House doesn't scrap the system and begin baking cookies for the enemy."

If the wrong person wins they may do just that, and that makes me a little nervous."

"At any rate, Kudos to the officers & Crew of the USS Lake Erie. Well done, blue jackets!!"

Funny, just last week Obama reiterated how when he's president he will stop all missile technology and push for nuclear disarmament.

If he were president now, we wouldn't even have been able to shoot that satellite down AND show the world that we CAN protect ourselves and will do so if the need arises.

Obama doesn't want the rest of the world threatened by the creepy US of A. Something to run through the think-0-matic before you vote.

THINK ABOUT IT

Can this be so??? Remembering helps!

I strongly urge each one of you to repost this as many times as you can!

Each opportunity that you have to send it to a friend...do it!

A lot of Americans have become so insulated from reality that they imagine that America can suffer defeat without any inconvenience to themselves. Pause a moment, reflect back. These events are actual events from history.

They really happened!

Do you remember?

1) 1968 Bobby Kennedy was shot and killed by Muslim male extremist between the ages of 17 and 40.

2) In 1972 at the Munich Olympics, athletes were kidnapped and massacred by Muslim male extremists between the ages of 17 and 40

3) In 1979, the US embassy in Iran was taken over by Muslim male extremists between the ages of 17 and 40

4) During the 1980's a number of Americans were kidnapped in Lebanon by Muslim male extremists between the ages of 17 and 40

5) In 1983, the US Marine barracks in Beirut was blown up by Muslim male extremists between the ages of 17 and 40

6) In 1985 the cruise ship Achille Lauro was hijacked and a 70 year old American passenger was murdered and thrown overboard in his wheelchair by Muslim male extremists between the ages of 17 and 40

7) In 1985 TWA flight 847 was hijacked at Athens, and a US Navy diver trying to rescue passengers was murdered by Muslim male extremists between the ages of 17 and 40

8) In 1988, Pan Am Flight 103 was bombed by Muslim male extremists between the ages of 17 and 40

9) In 1993 the World Trade Center was bombed the first time by Muslim male extremists between the ages of 17 and 40

10) In 1998, the US embassies in Kenya and Tanzania were bombed by Muslim male extremists between the ages of 17 and 40

11) On 9/11/01, four airliners were hijacked; two were used as missiles to take down the World Trade Centers and of the

remaining two, one crashed into the US Pentagon and the other was diverted and crashed by the passengers. Thousands of people were killed by Muslim male extremists between the ages of 17 and 40

12) In 2002 the United States fought a war in < /SPANAfghanistan against Muslim male extremists between the ages of 17 and 40

13) In 2002 reporter Daniel Pearl was kidnapped and murdered by--you guessed it--Muslim male extremists between the ages of 17 and 40

No, I really don't see a pattern here to justify profiling, do you? So, to ensure we Americans never offend anyone, particularly fanatic's intent on killing us, airport security screeners will no longer be allowed to profile certain people...Absolutely No Profiling!

They must conduct random searches of 80-year-old women, little kids, airline pilots with proper identification, secret agents who are members of the President's security detail, 85-year old Congressmen with metal hips, and Medal of Honor winner and former Governor Joe Foss, but leave Muslim Males between the ages 17 and 40 alone lest they be guilty of profiling.

According to The Book of Revelations:

The Anti-Christ will be a man, in his 40s, of MUSLIM descent, who will deceive the nations with persuasive language, and have a MASSIVE Christ-like appeal....the prophecy says that people will flock to him and he will promise false hope and world peace, and when he is in power, he will destroy everything.

And Now:

For the award winning Act of Stupidity; of all times the People of

America want to elect, to the most Powerful position on the face of the Planet--The Presidency of the United States of America A Muslim Male Extremist Between the ages of 17 and 40.

Have the American People completely lost their Minds, or just their Power of Reason?

I'm sorry but I refuse to take a chance on the 'unknown' candidate Obama...

Let's send this to as many people as we can so that the Gloria Allreds and other stupid attorneys along with Federal Justices that want to thwart common sense, feel ashamed of themselves -- if they have any such sense.

As the writer of the award winning story 'Forrest Gump' so aptly put it, 'Stupid Is As Stupid Does.'

STANLEY ANN DUNHAM – OBAMA'S MOTHER

Stanley Ann Dunham

Mercer Island High School

Stanley Ann Dunham Obama Soetoro (November 29, 1942 - November 7, 1995), known as Ann Dunham and Stanley Ann Dunham, was an American anthropologist, left-wing social activist, and the mother of Senator Obama Obama. She was born in Fort Leavenworth, Kansas, to Stanley and Madelyn Dunham. Her father (who gave his only child his name) was a furniture salesman in downtown Seattle, Washington, and her mother worked for a bank. After a year living in Seattle, her family moved to Mercer Island, Washington, in 1956 so that 13-year old Ann could attend the Mercer Island High School that had just opened. At the school she was on the debate team and graduated in 1960.

Her family moved to Hawaii and Ann attended the University of Hawaii at Manoa, where she studied anthropology. When Ann Dunham arrived in Hawaii, she was a fully fledged radical leftist and practitioner of 'critical theory' She also began to engage in miscegenation (inter-racial relationships) as part of her attack on society. Susan Blake, one of her friends has stated she never dated 'the crew-cut white boys,' She had a world view, even as a young girl. It was embracing the different, rather than that ethnocentric thing of shunning the different. That was where her mind took her. In Hawaii she met Obama Obama, Sr. from Kenya in her Russian 1 language class. Obama, Jr. was born August 4, 1961. Obama, Sr. left Ann and their son in 1963 to attend Harvard in Boston. Press reports claim Ann Dunham and Obama Sr. were divorced around this time; however, no evidence has yet been presented to show they were ever married. The senior Obama obtained a masters degree in economics at Harvard and returned to Kenya in 1965 where he obtained a position in the Kenyan government. He was killed in an automobile accident in 1982.

Two years later, when her son was five, Dunham married Lolo Soetoro, an Indonesian oil manager and practicing Muslim whom she meet at the university . In 1967 they moved to Jakarta, Indonesia. While in Indonesia Ann got a job at the American embassy teaching English. Obama's half-sister, Maya Soetoro was born in Indonesia. Ann, Obama and his sister Maya moved back to Hawaii. Ann Dunham soon returned to Indonesia with Maya but divorced Soetoro in the late 1970s.

Dunham traveled around the world, pursuing a career in rural development that took her to Ghana, India, Thailand, Indonesia, Nepal and Bangladesh. In 1986 Ann Dunham worked on a developmental project in Pakistan. Later that year Ann and her daughter traveled the Silk Road in China. In 1992 she earned a P h.D. in anthropology from the University of Hawaii. Her dissertation, 'Peasant blacksmithing in Indonesia: Surviving and Thriving Against All Odds,' was 1067 pages long. She worked for the Ford Foundation and promoted Micro lending.

During Obama's campaign for the 2008 presidential election he portrayed his mother as a Conservative girl from Kansas; however in reality she was a radical leftist and cultural Marxist. She lived in the Seattle area; spending her teenage years in Seattle's coffee shops with other young radical leftist. Obama claims his mother's family were Conservative Methodists or Baptists from Kansas. However his mother's parents were members of a left-wing Unitarian church near Seattle. The church located in Bellevue, Washington was nicknamed 'the little red church,' because of its communist leanings. The school Ann attended, Mercer Island High School, was a hotbed of pro-Marxist radical teachers. John Stenhouse, board member, told the House Un-American Activities Subcommittee that he had been a member of the Communist Party USA and this school has a number of Marxists on its staff. Two teachers at this school, Val Foubert and Jim Wichterman, both Frankfurt School style Marxists, taught a critical theory curriculum to students which included; rejection of societal norms, attacks on Christianity, the traditional family, and assigned readings by Karl Marx. The hallway between Foubert's and

Wichterman classrooms was sometimes called 'anarchy ally.'
Dunham has been described by her friends as 'a fellow traveler...'
meaning a communist sympathizer.

In an interview, Obama referred to his mother as 'the dominant
figure in my formative years...The values she taught me continue to
be my touchstone when it comes to how I go about the world of
politics.'

Before she died Ann Dunham wanted to adopt a mixed-race Korean
baby fathered by a Black American stationed in South Korea. Ann
Dunham died in Hawaii in 1995 of ovarian cancer and uterine
cancer.

MY PLEA TO REPUBLICANS

My plea to Republicans: it's time for real change to avoid real
disaster

The Republican loss in the special election for Louisiana's Sixth
Congressional District last Saturday should be a sharp wake up call
for Republicans: Either Congressional Republicans are going to
chart a bold course of real change or they are going to suffer decisive
losses this November.

The facts are clear and compelling.

Saturday's loss was in a district that President Bush carried by 19
percentage points in 2004 and that the Republicans have held since
1975.

This defeat follows on the loss of Speaker Hastert's seat in Illinois.
That seat had been held by a Republican for 76 years with the single
exception of the 1974 Watergate election when the Democrats held it

for one term. That same seat had been carried by President Bush 55-44% in 2004.

Two GOP Losses That Validate a National Pattern

These two special elections validate a national polling pattern that is bad news for Republicans. According to a New York Times/CBS Poll, Americans disapprove of the President's job performance by 63 to 28 (and he has been below 40% job approval since December 2006, the longest such period for any president in the history of polling).

A separate New York Times/CBS Poll shows that a full 81 percent of Americans believe the economy is on the wrong track.

The current generic ballot for Congress according to the NY Times/CBS poll is 50 to 32 in favor of the Democrats. That is an 18-point margin, reminiscent of the depths of the Watergate disaster.

Congressional Republicans Can't Take Comfort in McCain's Poll Numbers. Senator McCain is currently running ahead of the Republican Congressional ballot by about 16 percentage points. But there are two reasons that this extraordinary personal achievement should not comfort Congressional Republicans.

First, McCain's lead is a sign of the gap between the McCain brand of independence and the GOP brand. No regular Republican would be tying or slightly beating the Democratic candidates in this atmosphere. It is a sign of how much McCain is a non-traditional Republican that he is sustaining his personal popularity despite his party's collapse.

Second, there is a grave danger for the McCain campaign that if the generic ballot stays at only 32 % for the GOP it will ultimately outweigh McCain's personal appeal and drag his candidacy into defeat.

The Anti-Obama, Anti-Wright, and Anti-Clinton GOP Model Has Been Tested -- And It Failed

The Republican brand has been so badly damaged that if Republicans try to run an anti-Obama, anti- Reverend Wright, or (if Senator Clinton wins), anti-Clinton campaign, they are simply going to fail.

This model has already been tested with disastrous results.

In 2006, there were six incumbent Republican Senators who had plenty of money, the advantage of incumbency, and traditionally successful consultants.

But the voters in all six states had adopted a simple position: "Not you." No matter what the GOP Senators attacked their opponents with, the voters shrugged off the attacks and returned to, "Not you." The danger for House and Senate Republicans in 2008 is that the voters will say, "Not the Republicans." Republicans Have Lost the Advantage on Every Single-Issue Poll.

A February Washington Post poll shows that Republicans have lost the advantage to the Democrats on which party can handle an issue better -- on every single topic.

Americans now believe that Democrats can handle the deficit better (52 to 31), taxes better (48 to 40) and even terrorism better (44 to 37).

This is a catastrophic collapse of trust in Republicans built up over three generations on the deficit, two generations on taxes, and two generations on national security.

House Republicans Should Call an Emergency, Members-Only Conference.

Faced with these election results, the House Republicans should hold an emergency members-only meeting. At the meeting, they should pose this stark choice: Real change or certain defeat.

If a majority of the House Republicans vote for real change, they should instruct Republican Leader John Boehner and his team to come back with a new plan by the Wednesday before the Memorial Day recess. This plan should involve real change in legislative, communications, and campaign strategy and involve immediate, real action, including a complete overhaul of the Congressional Campaign Committee. The House Republican Conference would then vote for the plan or insist on its revision.

If a majority of the House Republicans are opposed to acting then the minority who are activists should establish a parallel organization dedicated to real change. This group should focus its energies on creating the changes necessary to survive despite a conference with a minority mindset that accepts defeat rather than fights for real change (which is what we had when I entered Congress in 1978).

Nine Acts of Real Change That Could Restore the GOP Brand

Here are nine acts of real change that would begin to rebuild the American people's confidence that Republicans share their values, understand their worries, and are prepared to act instead of just talk. The Republicans in Congress could get a start on all nine this week if they had the will to do so.

1) Repeal the gas tax for the summer, and pay for the repeal by cutting domestic discretionary spending so that the transportation infrastructure trust fund would not be hurt. At a time when, according to The Hill newspaper, Senator Clinton is asking for $2.3billion in earmarks, it should be possible for Republicans to establish a "government spending versus your pocketbook" fight over cutting the gas tax that would resonate with most Americans. Lower taxes and less government spending should be a battle cry most taxpayers and all Conservatives could rally behind.

2) Redirect the oil being put into the national petroleum reserve onto the open market. That oil would lower the price of gasoline an extra 5 to 6 cents per gallon, and its sale would lower the deficit.

3) Introduce a "more energy at lower cost with less environmental damage and greater national security bill" as a replacement for the Warner-Lieberman "tax and trade" bill which is coming to the floor of the Senate in the next few weeks (see my newsletter next week for an outline of a solid pro-economy, pro-national security, pro-environment energy bill). When the American people realize how much the current energy prices are actually a "politicians' energy crisis" they will demand real change in our policies.

4) Establish an earmark moratorium for one year and pledge to uphold the presidential veto of bills with earmarks through the end of 2009. The American people are fed up with politicians spending their money. They currently believe both parties are

equally bad. This is a real opportunity to show the difference.

5) Overhaul the census and cut its budget radically. The recent announcement that the Census Bureau could not build an effective hand-held computer for $1.3 billion and is turning instead to 600,000 temporary workers to do a paper and pencil census in 2010 is an opportunity to slash its budget, shrink its bureaucracy, and turn to entrepreneurial internet-based companies to build an information-age census. This is an absurdity that cries out for bold, decisive reform (see my YouTube video "FedEx versus federal bureaucracy" for an example of what I mean).

6) Implement a space-based, GPS-style air traffic control system. The problems of the Federal Aviation Administration are symptoms of a union-dominated bureaucracy resisting change. If we implemented a space-based GPS-style air traffic system we would get 40% more air travel with one-half the bureaucrats. The union has stopped 200,000,000 passengers from enjoying more reliable air travel to protect 7,000 obsolete jobs. This real change would allow the millions of frustrated travelers to have champions in Congress trying to help them get places better, safer, faster.

7) Declare English the official language of government. This real change is supported by 91% of the American people including a majority of Democrats, Republicans, Independents, and Latinos. It is an issue of national unity that brings Americans together in a red, white, and blue majority.

8) Protect the workers' right to a secret ballot. The vast majority

(around 81%) of Americans believe that American workers have a right to have a secret ballot election before they are forced to join a union. Last year the House Democrats passed a bill that would strip American workers of the secret ballot. A new bill should be introduced reaffirming that right, and it should be brought up again and again until marginal Democrats are forced to vote with the American people against the union power structure.

9) Remind Americans that judge's matter. Senate Republicans should mount an ongoing fight (including a filibuster of other activities if necessary) to get the American people to realize that Liberals want to block all current judicial appointments in order to maximize the number of left wing radical judges they can appoint if they win the White House. This issue has three advantages. It reminds people that judges matter and that a leftwing radical Supreme Court would be bad for the values of most (70 to 90 percent, depending on the issue) Americans. It shows the Democrats are not engaged in fair play. It arouses the activism of those who have been disappointed by Republicans and have forgotten how bad a Liberal Democratic Presidency would be.

What Is at Stake:

No Republicans should kid themselves. It's time to face up to a stark choice.

Without change we could face a catastrophic election this fall.

Without change the Republican Party in the House could revert to the permanent minority status it had from 1930 to 1994.

Without change, the majorities of Americans who support the Republican principle of smaller, more efficient, smarter and fairer government will be in for a rude awakening. It's time for real change to avoid a real disaster.

The "May Day Massacre": Can Liberals Govern in a Global Economy?

Despite the poor outlook for Conservatives in our elections this November, there is encouraging news from across the Atlantic. The Conservative wave sweeping Europe hit England last week when the Liberal Labor Party suffered its worst local election results in 40 years.

Boris Johnson became the first Conservative Party member elected mayor of London when he defeated Labour candidate "Red" Ken Livingstone. In contests for more than 4,000 local seats across England, Conservatives captured 44 percent of the vote, compared to 25 percent for the Liberal Democrats and just 24 percent for Labour. This Conservative victory in England comes on the heels of a history-making rout of the Communists and the Greens in parliamentary elections in Italy two weeks ago. And the Italian results

follow center-right victories in France (Sarkozy) and Germany (Merkel). The countries of so-called "old" Europe are turning away from the Liberal high tax, big government policies that have crippled their economies and are turning toward pro-growth, pro-competitive center-right solutions.

All of which raises the question: Can the Left successfully govern in a modern, global economy? The voters of Europe are saying no.

WISH WE HAD MORE LIKE THIS IN THE US

The recently elected mayor of Doncaster, in South Yorkshire, has infuriated Britain's politically powerful homosexualist lobby by attempting to withhold local funding for this year's Gay Pride celebrations. The funding for this year's event in June went through, but Mayor Peter Davies, a member of the English Democrat party and the father of Tory MP Philip Davies, has scrapped all future funding for the annual Gay Pride event.

"I'm not a homophobe," he said, "but I don't see why council taxpayers should pay to celebrate anyone's sexuality."

Davies is only the second mayor of Doncaster to have been elected directly by a popular vote rather than by council members. He campaigned on a popular platform, that has reportedly alarmed the political classes on both the Labour and Tory sides of the House, in which he pledged to "stamp out political correctness" in every area of Doncaster's local government.

To accomplish this, Davies has recruited the group Campaign Against Political Correctness (CAPC) to consult on his planned reforms. A spokesman for the CAPC, John Midgley, said that "people are crying out" for an end to the wave of politically correct policies in Britain. "We commissioned a survey by ICM," Midgley said, "that said 80 per cent of people are fed up to the back teeth with it."

Davies promised to end council funding for "politically correct initiatives" and to "scrap politically correct non-jobs" such as "community cohesion officers" and "encourage the former employees to seek meaningful employment."

In his first week in office, Davies fulfilled his promises by cutting his own salary from £73,000 to £30,000; reducing the number of councilors from 63 to 21 and saving the town £800,000 a year. He immediately announced plans to reduce council tax by 3 per cent and got rid of the mayoral limousine. He ended a "twinning" arrangement with five towns around the world, which he described as "just for people to fly off and have a binge at the council's expense."

While campaigning earlier this year, and in the midst of a national pandemic of violent youth crime, Davies, who is a retired school teacher, called for harsher punishments for "young thugs." As a founding member of the Campaign for Real Education, Davies has pressed for restoration of traditional methods in schools that he says will reduce crime and restore Britain's once-legendary public order. He also called on the government to withdraw Britain from the European Union "in order to save billions of pounds each year and return control of the country's affairs to our own parliament."

Calling him the UK's "most gloriously un-PC" mayor, the Daily Mail's Robert Hardman asked, "Who should be most worried about his success: Labour or the Tories? Because his message threatens both."

Hardman commented, "To the shock and dismay of many local councilors and MPs, most of Westminster and the entire Government, the assiduously straight-talking Mr. Davies has just become one of the most powerful politicians in Britain."

Columnist and pundit Gerald Warner, writing for the Daily Telegraph's blog, called Davies's tenure "the beginning of the end for political correctness" and a sign that "the counter-revolution has begun." His agenda, Warner wrote, "against all the tenets of consensual British politics, consists of doing what the public wants."

THIS IS DISTURBING

A San Francisco
cosmetics company has ignited an outcry among pro-lifers for including an unexpected ingredient in its anti-aging creams: skin-cell proteins from an aborted fetus.
Children of God for Life
a watchdog group that monitors the use of fetal material in medical products, called last week for a boycott of all treatments manufactured by Neocutis Inc., which acknowledges that the key ingredient in its product line was developed from an aborted boy.
"There's just no excuse for using aborted babies in skin-care products," said Debi Vinnedge, executive director of Children of God for Life
a 10-year-old organization based in Murfreesboro, Tenn. "The reaction, the shock and anger I've seen is incredible."
In a statement released Friday, in response to a wave of condemnation from pro-life and religious blogs, Neocutis defended the use of its trademarked ingredient, Processed Skin Cell Proteins, or PSP, arguing that the fetal cell line was harvested in a responsible, ethical manner for use in treating severe dermatological injuries.
The company compared its situation to that of researchers who used fetal kidney cells to develop the polio vaccine.
"Our view - which is shared by most medical professionals and

patients - is that the limited, prudent and responsible use of donated fetal skin tissue can continue to ease suffering, speed healing, save lives and improve the well-being of many patients around the globe," said the statement.

The ingredient was developed at the University of Lausanne in Switzerland from proteins in the skin tissue of a 14-week-old male baby electively aborted at the university's hospital and donated to the Swiss university. The abortion was deemed medically necessary because the baby could not survive to term, according to Neocutis. The fetal skin cell line was taken from a piece of skin the size of a postage stamp and donated voluntarily by the parents for medical research. The donation was approved by the hospital's medical ethics committee and in accordance with Swiss laws, said the Neocutis statement.

Neocutis also insisted that the one donation would be sufficient for the manufacture of its products. Critics argue that it's impossible to know how long the cell line will last, but Neocutis states on its Web site that "no additional fetal biopsies will ever be required."

"We feel we are in complete compliance with the laws of God and the laws of man," Neocutis President Mark J. Lemko said in an e-mail response to critics, which was posted on the Children of God for Life web site.

WHY MLK WAS A REPUBLICAN

Why Martin Luther King Was Republican

It should come as no surprise that Dr. Martin Luther King, Jr. was a Republican. In that era, almost all black Americans were

Republicans. Why? From its founding in 1854 as the anti-slavery party until today, the Republican Party has championed freedom and civil rights for blacks. And as one pundit so succinctly stated, the Democrat Party is as it always has been, the party of the four S's: slavery, secession, segregation and now socialism.

It was the Democrats who fought to keep blacks in slavery and passed the discriminatory Black Codes and Jim Crow laws. The Democrats started the Ku Klux Klan to lynch and terrorize blacks. The Democrats fought to prevent the passage of every civil rights law beginning with the civil rights laws of the 1860s, and continuing with the civil rights laws of the 1950s and 1960s.

During the civil rights era of the 1960s, Dr. King was fighting the Democrats who stood in the school house doors, turned skin-burning fire hoses on blacks and let loose vicious dogs. It was Republican President Dwight Eisenhower who pushed to pass the Civil Rights Act of 1957 and sent troops to Arkansas to desegregate schools. President Eisenhower also appointed Chief Justice Earl Warren to the U.S. Supreme Court, which resulted in the 1954 Brown v. Board of Education decision ending school segregation. Much is made of Democrat President Harry Truman's issuing an Executive Order in 1948 to desegregate the military. Not mentioned is the fact that it was Eisenhower who actually took action to effectively end segregation in the military.

Democrat President John F. Kennedy is lauded as a proponent of civil rights. However, Kennedy voted against the 1957 Civil Rights Act while he was a senator, as did Democrat Sen. Al Gore Sr. And after he became President, Kennedy was opposed to the 1963 March on Washington by Dr. King that was organized by A. Phillip Randolph, who was a black Republican. President Kennedy, through his brother Atty. Gen. Robert Kennedy, had Dr. King wiretapped and investigated by the FBI on suspicion of being a Communist in order to undermine Dr. King.

In March of 1968, while referring to Dr. King's leaving Memphis, Tenn., after riots broke out where a teenager was killed, Democrat Sen. Robert Byrd (W.Va.), a former member of the Ku Klux Klan, called Dr. King a "trouble-maker" who starts trouble, but runs like a coward after trouble is ignited. A few weeks later, Dr. King returned to Memphis and was assassinated on April 4, 1968.

Given the circumstances of that era, it is understandable why Dr. King was a Republican. It was the Republicans who fought to free blacks from slavery and amended the Constitution to grant blacks freedom (13th Amendment), citizenship (14th Amendment) and the right to vote (15th Amendment). Republicans passed the civil rights laws of the 1860s, including the Civil Rights Act of 1866 and the Reconstruction Act of 1867 that was designed to establish a new government system in the Democrat-controlled South, one that was fair to blacks. Republicans also started the NAACP and affirmative action with Republican President Richard Nixon's 1969 Philadelphia Plan (crafted by black Republican Art Fletcher) that set the nation's fist goals and timetables. Although affirmative action now has been turned by the Democrats into an unfair quota system, affirmative action was begun by Nixon to counter the harm caused to blacks when Democrat President Woodrow Wilson in 1912 kicked all of the blacks out of federal government jobs.

Few black Americans know that it was Republicans who founded the Historically Black Colleges and Universities. Unknown also is the fact that Republican Sen. Everett Dirksen from Illinois was key to the passage of civil rights legislation in 1957, 1960, 1964 and 1965. Not mentioned in recent media stories about extension of the 1965 Voting Rights Act is the fact that Dirksen wrote the language for the bill. Dirksen also crafted the language for the Civil Rights Act of 1968 which prohibited discrimination in housing. President Lyndon Johnson could not have achieved passage of civil rights legislation without the support of Republicans.

Critics of Republican Sen. Barry Goldwater, who ran for President against Johnson in 1964, ignore the fact that Goldwater wanted to force the Democrats in the South to stop passing discriminatory laws and thus end the need to continuously enact federal civil rights legislation.

Those who wrongly criticize Goldwater also ignore the fact that Johnson, in his 4,500 State of the Union Address delivered on Jan. 4, 1965, mentioned scores of topics for federal action, but only 35 words were devoted to civil rights. He did not mention one word about voting rights. Then in 1967, showing his anger with Dr. King's protest against the Vietnam War, Johnson referred to Dr. King as "that Nigger preacher."

Contrary to the false assertions by Democrats, the racist "Dixiecrats" did not all migrate to the Republican Party. "Dixiecrats" declared that they would rather vote for a "yellow dog" than vote for a Republican because the Republican Party was known as the party for blacks. Today, some of those "Dixiecrats" continue their political careers as Democrats, including Robert Byrd, who is well known for having been a "Keagle" in the Ku Klux Klan.

Another former "Dixiecrat" is former Democrat Sen. Ernest Hollings, who put up the Confederate flag over the state Capitol when he was the governor of South Carolina. There was no public outcry when Democrat Sen. Christopher Dodd praised Byrd as someone who would have been "a great senator for any moment," including the Civil War. Yet Democrats denounced then-Senate GOP leader Trent Lott for his remarks about Sen. Strom Thurmond (R.-S.C.). Thurmond was never in the Ku Klux Klan and defended blacks against lynching and the discriminatory poll taxes imposed on blacks by Democrats. If Byrd and Thurmond were alive during the Civil War, and Byrd had his way, Thurmond would have been lynched.

The 30-year odyssey of the South switching to the Republican Party began in the 1970s with President Richard Nixon's "Southern Strategy," which was an effort on the part of Nixon to get Christians in the South to stop voting for Democrats who did not share their values and were still discriminating against their fellow Christians who happened to be black. Georgia did not switch until 2002, and some Southern states, including Louisiana, are still controlled by Democrats.

Today, Democrats, in pursuit of their socialist agenda, are fighting to keep blacks poor, angry and voting for Democrats. Examples of how egregiously Democrats act to keep blacks in poverty are numerous. After wrongly convincing black Americans that a minimum wage increase was a good thing, the Democrats on August 3 kept their promise and killed the minimum wage bill passed by House Republicans on July 29. The blockage of the minimum wage bill was the second time in as many years that Democrats stuck a legislative finger in the eye of black Americans. Senate Democrats on April 1, 2004, blocked passage of a bill to renew the 1996 welfare reform law that was pushed by Republicans and vetoed twice by President Clinton before he finally signed it. Since the welfare reform law expired in September 2002, Congress had passed six extensions, and the latest expired on June 30, 2004. Opposed by the Democrats are school choice opportunity scholarships that would help black children get out of failing schools and Social Security reform, even though blacks on average lose $10,000 in the current system because of a shorter life expectancy than whites (72.2 years for blacks vs. 77.5 years for whites).

Democrats have been running our inner-cities for the past 30 to 40 years, and blacks are still complaining about the same problems. More than $7 trillion dollars have been spent on poverty programs since Lyndon Johnson's War on Poverty with little, if any, impact on poverty. Diabolically, every election cycle, Democrats blame Republicans for the deplorable conditions in the inner-cities, then incite blacks to cast a protest vote against Republicans.

In order to break the Democrats' stranglehold on the black vote and free black Americans from the Democrat Party's economic plantation, we must shed the light of truth on the Democrats. We must demonstrate that the Democrat Party policies of socialism and dependency on government handouts offer the pathway to poverty, while Republican Party principles of hard work, personal responsibility, getting a good education and ownership of homes and small businesses offer the pathway to prosperity.

BORN 1776 - DIED 2008

Born 1776, Died 2008

It does not hurt to read this several times

Professor Joseph Olson of Hemline University School of Law, St. Paul , Minnesota , points out some interesting facts concerning the Presidential election:

- Number of States won by: Democrats: 19   Republicans: 29
- Square miles of land won by: Democrats: 580,000
    Republicans: 2,427,000
- Population of counties won by: Democrats: 127 million
    Republicans: 143 million
- Murder rate per 100,000 residents in counties won by:
    Democrats: 13.2   Republicans: 2.1

Professor Olson adds: "In aggregate, the map of the territory Republicans won was mostly the land owned by the taxpaying citizens of the country.

Democrat territory mostly encompassed those citizens living in government-owned tenements and living off various forms of government welfare..."

Olson believes the United States is now somewhere between the "complacency and apathy" phase of Professor Tyler's definition of democracy, with some forty percent of the nation's population already having reached the "governmental dependency" phase.

If Congress grants amnesty and citizenship to twenty million criminal invaders called illegals and they vote, then we can say goodbye to the USA in fewer than five years.

If you are in favor of this, then by all means, delete this message.

If you are not, then pass this along to help everyone realize just how much is at stake, knowing that apathy is the greatest danger to our freedom.

JOE LEGAL VS. JOSÉ LEGAL

The "Manchurian Candidate" has taken the reins of power

Joe legal vs. Jose illegal

You have two families: "Joe Legal" and "Jose Illegal". Both families have two parents, two children, and live in California.

Joe Legal works in construction, has a Social Security Number and makes $25.00 per hour with taxes deducted.

Jose Illegal also works in construction, has NO Social Security Number, and gets paid $15.00 cash "under the table".

Ready? Now pay attention...

Joe Legal: $25.00 per hour x 40 hours = $1000.00 per week, or $52,000.00 per year. Now take 30% away for state and federal tax; Joe Legal now has $31,231.00.

Jose Illegal: $15.00 per hour x 40 hours = $600.00 per week, or $31,200.00 per year. Jose Illegal pays no taxes. Jose Illegal now has $31,200.00.

Joe Legal pays medical and dental insurance with limited coverage for his family at $600.00 per month, or $7,200.00 per year. Joe Legal now has $24,031.00.

Jose Illegal has full medical and dental coverage through the state and local clinics at a cost of $0.00 per year. Jose Illegal still has $31,200.00.

Joe Legal makes too much money and is not eligible for food stamps or welfare. Joe Legal pays $500.00 per month for food, or $6,000.00 per year. Joe Legal now has $18,031.00.

Jose Illegal has no documented income and is eligible for food stamps and welfare. Jose Illegal still has $31,200.00.

Joe Legal pays rent of $1,200.00 per month, or $14,400.00 per year. Joe Legal now has $9,631.00.

Jose Illegal receives a $500.00 per month federal rent subsidy. Jose Illegal pays out that $500.00 per month, or $6,000.00 per year. Jose Illegal still has $ 31,200.00.

Joe Legal pays $200.00 per month, or $2,400.00 for insurance. Joe Legal now has $7,231.00.

Jose Illegal says, "We don't need no stinkin' insurance!" and still has $31,200.00.

Joe Legal has to make his $7,231.00 stretch to pay utilities, gasoline, etc.

Jose Illegal has to make his $31,200.00 stretch to pay utilities, gasoline, and what he sends out of the country every month.

Joe Legal now works overtime on Saturdays or gets a part time job after work.

Jose Illegal has nights and weekends off to enjoy with his family.

Joe Legal's and Jose Illegal's children both attend the same school. Joe Legal pays for his children's lunches while Jose Illegal's children get a government sponsored lunch. Jose Illegal's children have an after school ESL program. Joe Legal's children go home.

Joe Legal and Jose Illegal both enjoy the same police and fire services, but Joe paid for them and Jose did not pay.

Do you get it, now?

If you vote for or support any politician that supports illegal aliens...

THE HAIRCUT

One day a florist went to a barber for a haircut.

After the cut, he asked about his bill, and the barber replied, 'I cannot accept money from you, I'm doing community service this week.'

The florist was pleased and left the shop.

When the barber went to open his shop the next morning, there was a 'thank you' card and a dozen roses waiting for him at his door.

Later, a cop comes in for a haircut, and when he tries to pay his bill, the barber again replied, 'I cannot accept money from you, I'm doing community service this week.' The cop was happy and left the shop.

The next morning when the barber went to open up, there was a 'thank you' card and a dozen donuts waiting for him at his door.

Then a Congressman came in for a haircut, and when he went to pay his bill, the barber again replied, 'I cannot accept money from you. I'm doing community service this week.' The Congressman was very happy and left the shop.

The next morning, when the barber went to open up, there were a dozen Congressmen lined up waiting for a free haircut.

And that, my friends, illustrates the fundamental difference between the citizens of our country and the politicians who run it.

THOUGHT YOU WOULD LIKE TO KNOW

Nancy D'Alesandro was born in 1940. Like many slimy politicians, she was involved at an early age: her father was Thomas D'Alesandro, a U.S. Congressman from Baltimore and a mayor of Baltimore.

She graduated from Institute of Notre Dame, a Catholic all-girls school in Baltimore. She then attended Trinity College - another Roman Catholic institution. It was here that she got her claws into her future rich husband, Paul Frank Pelosi.

There is no mention in any of her bio material of what she studied or how she did academically. I can find no mention of her ever having a real job. Instead, she started as a political intern right out of college - a job her father got her, no doubt.

She interned for Senator Daniel Brewster. He was indicted in 1969 for a felony charge of accepting bribes. She also married Paul Frank Pelosi about this time (in 1963, at age 23). So far, this woman has done nothing at all and has not earned an honest dime of money in her life. Let's continue...

Paul and Nancy moved to San Francisco in 1969 where...surprise of surprises, Paul's brother (Ronald Pelosi) was heavily involved in city and county politics. She also buddied up with Phillip Burton (U.S. Congressman, 5th Dist - and brother of John L. Burton, CA State Senator and also a U.S. Congressman).

Another pause...

Are you starting to get a sense of how clubby and nepotistic the entire field of politics is? Most people really have no idea. If you think the smartest and most able are drawn to this field, you are completely off the mark. American politics is filled with inbred idiots and cretins galore - much like monarchies past. Let's continue...

Burton croaked in 1983 and threw his wife Sala in there (more nepotism). Then Sala got cancer and picked Pelosi as her successor. Talk about a piece of luck! She was then elected in a special session to the safest Congressional seat in the country (Democrats have held this seat since 1949 and Republicans make up 13% of the voters in the district).

Since her initial victory in 1987, she has been re-elected 10 times, receiving at least 75% of the vote and has never participated in candidate debates.

So this woman was essentially handed a seat by the previous office-holder and since it is the safest seat in the country, she has gotten to sit back on her ass and never lower herself to even discussing any issues with other candidates.

Now, Nancy ranks second in the line of presidential succession. She is also the lead blabbermouth on all the bailout and stimulus talks. She is the one constantly telling the nation we need to spend $500 billion more sending checks to people.

I say that again...she is in charge of how hundreds of billions of dollars is being spent and she has never held a real job, owned a business, or earned a dime in her life in the private sector.

In short, there is no proof she knows anything more about economics, finance or business than my 9-year-old niece. She was born and bred to be a rich guy's wife (the Pelosi family has a net worth of about $20 million and she is constantly among the richest members in Congress). Her rich husband got her a nice little job playing in San Francisco politics to give her something to do all day, and now she is two heart beats away from the presidency.

That should scare the shit out of you.

OBAMA THE IDIOT...

Bad press, including major mockery of the plan by comedian Jon Stewart, led to President Obama abandoning his proposal to require veterans carry private health insurance to cover the estimated $540 million annual cost to the federal government of treatment for injuries to military personnel received during their tours on active duty. The President admitted that he was puzzled by the magnitude of the opposition to his proposal.

"Look, it's an all volunteer force," Obama complained. "Nobody made these guys go to war. They had to have known and accepted the risks. Now they whine about bearing the costs of their choice? It doesn't compute.." "I thought these were people who were proud to sacrifice for their country, "Obama continued. "I wasn't asking for blood, just money. With the country facing the worst financial crisis in its history, I'd have thought that the patriotic thing to do would be to try to help reduce the nation's deficit. I guess I underestimated the selfishness of some of my fellow Americans."

Please pass this on to everyone including every vet and their families whom you know.

How in the world did a person with this mindset become our leader? I didn't vote for him!!!

Remember this statement..."Nobody made these guys go to war. They had to have known and accepted the risks. Now they whine about bearing the costs of their choice?

If this person thinks he will ever get another vote from an Active Duty, Reserve, National Guard service member or veteran of a military service he ought to think it over. If you or a family member is or has served their country please pass this to them. Please pass this to everyone. I'm guessing that other than the 20-25 percent hardcore Liberals in the US will agree that this is just another example why this is the worst president in American history. Remind everyone over and over how this man thinks, while he bows to the Saudi Arabian king.

WELL SAID!

This woman is right on the money. This letter you are about to read was written by a 4th grade teacher. She even gave the world her telephone and fax numbers. We are in dire need of more true American citizens who are proud of our United States of America.

The White House

1600 Pennsylvania Avenue NW

Washington, DC 20500

Mr. Obama:

I have had it with you and your administration, sir. Your conduct on your recent trip overseas has convinced me that you are not an adequate representative of the United States of America collectively or of me personally.

You are so obsessed with appeasing the Europeans and the Muslim world that you have abdicated the responsibilities of the President of the United States of America. You are responsible to the citizens of the United States.

You are not responsible to the peoples of any other country on earth. I personally resent that you go around the world apologizing for the United States telling Europeans that we are arrogant and do not care about their status in the world. Sir, what do you think the First World War and the Second World War were all about if not the consideration of the peoples of Europe? Are you brain dead? What do you think the Marshall Plan was all about?

Do you not understand or know the history of the 20th century? Where do you get off telling a Muslim country that the United States does not consider itself a Christian country? Have you not read the Declaration of Independence or the Constitution of the United States? This country was founded on Judeo-Christian ethics and the principles governing this country, at least until you came along, come directly from this heritage. Do you not understand this?

Your bowing to the king of Saudi Arabia is an affront to all Americans. Our President does not bow down to anyone, let alone the king of Saudi Arabia. You don't show Great Britain, our best and one of our oldest allies, the respect they deserve yet you bow down to the king of Saudi Arabia. How dare you, sir! How dare you!

You can't find the time to visit the graves of our greatest generation because you don't want to offend the Germans but make time to visit a mosque in Turkey. You offended our dead and every veteran when you give the Germans more respect than the people who saved the German people from themselves. What's the matter with you?

I am convinced that you and the members of your administration have the historical and intellectual depth of a mud puddle and should be ashamed of yourselves, all of you. You are so self-righteously offended by the big bankers and the American automobile manufacturers yet do nothing about the real thieves in this situation, Mr. Dodd, Mr. Frank, Franklin Raines, Jamie Gorelic, the Fannie Mae bonuses, and the Freddie Mac bonuses. What do you intend to do about them? Anything? I seriously doubt it.

What about the U.S. House members passing out $9.1 million in bonuses to their staff members - on top of the $2.5 million in automatic pay raises those lawmakers gave themselves? I understand the average House aide got a 17% bonus. I took a 5% cut in my pay to save jobs with my employer.

You haven't said anything about that. Who authorized that? I surely didn't! Executives at Fannie Mae and Freddie Mac will be receiving $210 million in bonuses over an eighteen-month period, that's $45 million more than the AIG bonuses. In fact, Fannie and Freddie executives have already been awarded $51 million - not a bad take. Who authorized that and why haven't you expressed your outrage at this group who are largely responsible for the economic mess we have right now.

I resent that you take me and my fellow citizens as brain-dead and not caring about what you idiots do. We are watching what you are doing and we are getting increasingly fed up with all of you. I also want you to know that I personally find just about everything you do and say to be offensive to every one of my sensibilities. I promise you that I will work tirelessly to see that you do not get a chance to spend two terms destroying my beautiful country.

Sincerely,

Every Real American

P.S. I rarely ask that emails be 'passed around'...

Please send this to your email list...its past time for all Americans to wake up!

Who Am I?

I was born in one country, raised in another. My father was born in another country. I was not his only child. He fathered several children with numerous women.

I became very close to my mother, as my father showed no interest in me. My mother died at an early age from cancer.

Later in life, questions arose over my real name.

My birth records were sketchy and no one was able to produce a legitimate, reliable birth certificate.

I grew up practicing one faith but converted to Christianity, as it was widely accepted in my country, but I practiced non-traditional beliefs & didn't follow Christianity, except in the public eye under scrutiny.

I worked and lived among lower-class people as a young adult, disguising myself as someone who really cared about them.

That was before I decided it was time to get serious about my life and I embarked on a new career.

I wrote a book about my struggles growing up. It was clear to those who read my memoirs that I had difficulties accepting that my father abandoned me as a child.

I became active in local politics in my 30's then with help behind the scenes, I literally burst onto the scene as a candidate for national office in my 40s. They said I had a golden tongue and could talk anyone into anything. That reinforced my conceit.

I had a virtually non-existent resume, little work history, and no experience in leading a single organization. Yet I was a powerful speaker and citizens were drawn to me as though I were a magnet and they were small roofing tacks.

I drew incredibly large crowds during my public appearances. This bolstered my ego.

At first, my political campaign focused on my country's foreign policy. I was very critical of my country in the last war and seized every opportunity to bash my country.

But what launched my rise to national prominence were my views on the country's economy. I pretended to have a really good plan on how we could do better and every poor person would be fed and housed for free.

I knew which group was responsible for getting us into this mess. It was the free market, banks and corporations. I decided to start making citizens hate them and if they were envious of others who did well, the plan was clinched tight.

I called mine "A People's Campaign" and that sounded good to all people.

I was the surprise candidate because I emerged from outside the traditional path of politics and was able to gain widespread popular support.

I knew that, if I merely offered the people 'hope', together we could change our country and the world.

So, I started to make my speeches sound like they were on behalf of the downtrodden, poor, ignorant to include "persecuted minorities" like the Jews. My true views were not widely known & I needed to keep them unknown, until after I became my nation's leader.

I had to carefully guard reality, as anybody could have easily found out what I really believed, if they had simply read my writings and examined those people I associated with.

I'm glad they didn't. Then I became the most powerful man in the world. And the world learned the truth.

Who am I? *

Adolf Hitler

Who were you thinking of?

Scary isn't it?

READ #8 CAREFULLY...

Dear Senator Frist:

There is a huge amount of propaganda and myths circulating about illegal aliens, particularly illegal Mexican, Salvadorian, Guatemalan and Honduran aliens.

1) Illegal aliens generally do NOT want U.S. citizenship. Americans are very vain thinking that everybody in the world wants to be a U.S. citizen. Mexicans, and other nationalities want to remain citizens of their home countries while obtaining the benefits offered by the United States such as employment, medical care, in-state tuition, and government subsidized housing and free education for their offspring. Their main attraction is employment and their loyalty usually remains at home. They want benefits earned and subsidized by middle class

Americans. What illegal aliens want are benefits of American residence without paying the price.

2) There are no jobs that Americans won't do. Illegal aliens are doing jobs that Americans can't take and still support their families. Illegal aliens take low wage jobs, live dozens in a single residence home, share expenses and send money to their home country. There are no jobs that Americans won't do for a decent wage.

3) Every person who illegally entered this nation left a home. They are not homeless and they are not Americans. Some left jobs in their home countries. They come to send money to their real home as evidenced by the more than 20 billion dollars sent out of the country each year by illegal aliens. These illegal aliens knowingly and willfully entered this nation in violation of the law and therefore assumed the risk of detection and deportation. Those who brought their alien children assumed the responsibility and risk on behalf of their children.

4) Illegal aliens are not critical to the economy. Illegal aliens constitute less than 5% of the workforce. However, they reduce wages and benefits for lawful U.S. residents.

5) This is not an immigrant nation. There are 280 million native born Americans. While it is true that this nation was settled and founded by immigrants (legal immigrants), it is also true that there is not a nation on this planet that was not settled by immigrants at one time or another.

6) The United States is welcoming to legal immigrants. Illegal aliens are not immigrants by definition. The U.S. accepts more

lawful immigrants every year than the rest of the world combined.

7) There is no such thing as the "Hispanic vote". Hispanics are white, brown, black and every shade in between. Hispanics are Republicans, Democrats, Anarchists, Communists, Marxists and Independents. The so-called "Hispanic vote" is a myth. Pandering to illegal aliens to get the Hispanic vote is a dead end.

8) Mexico is not a friend of the United States. Since 1848 Mexicans have resented the United States. During World War I Mexico allowed German Spies to operate freely in Mexico to spy on the U.S. During World War II Mexico allowed the Axis powers to spy on the U.S. from Mexico. During the Cold War Mexico allowed spies hostile to the U.S. to operate freely. The attack on the Twin Towers in 2001 was cheered and applauded all across Mexico. Today Mexican school children are taught that the U.S. stole California , Arizona , New Mexico and Texas. If you don't believe it, check out some Mexican textbooks written for their schoolchildren.

9) Although some illegal aliens enter this country for a better life, there are 6 billion people on this planet. At least 1 billion of those live on less than one dollar a day. If wanting a better life is a valid excuse to break the law and sneak into America, then let's allow those one billion to come to America and we'll turn the USA into a Third World nation overnight. Besides, there are 280 million native born Americans who want a better life. I'll bet Bill Gates and Donald Trump want a better life. When will the USA lifeboat be full? Since when is wanting a better life a good

reason to trash another nation?

10) There is a labor shortage in this country. This is a lie. There are hundreds of thousands, if not millions, of American housewives, senior citizens, students, unemployed and underemployed who would gladly take jobs at a decent wage.

11) It is racist to want secure borders. What is racist about wanting secure borders and a secure America ? What is racist about not wanting people to sneak into America and steal benefits we have set aside for legal aliens, senior citizens, children and other legal residents? What is it about race that entitles people to violate our laws, steal identities, and take the American Dream without paying the price?

For about four decades American politicians have refused to secure our borders and look after the welfare of middle class Americans. These politicians have been of both parties. A huge debt to American society has resulted. This debt will be satisfied and the interest will be high. There have already been riots in the streets by illegal aliens and their supporters. There will be more. You, as a politician, have a choice to offend the illegal aliens who have stolen into this country and demanded the rights afforded to U.S. citizens or to offend those of us who are stakeholders in this country. The interest will be steep either way.

There will be civil unrest. There will be a reckoning. Do you have the courage to do what is right for America ? Or, will you bow to the wants and needs of those who don't even have the right to remain here?

There will be a reckoning. It will come in November of this year, again in 2008 and yet again in 2010.

We will not allow America to be stolen by third world agitators and thieves.

SOMETHING TO THINK ABOUT...NBA OR NFL?

36 have been accused of spousal abuse

7 have been arrested for fraud

19 have been accused of writing bad checks

117 have directly or indirectly bankrupted at least 2 businesses

3 have done time for assault

71, repeat 71, cannot get a credit card due to bad credit

14 have been arrested on drug-related charges

8 have been arrested for shoplifting

21 currently are defendants in lawsuits

84 have been arrested for drunk driving in the last year

Can you guess which organization this is?

Give up yet?

Neither.

It's the 535 members of the United States Congress.

The same group of Idiots that crank out hundreds of new laws each year designed to keep the rest of us in line.

You gotta pass this one on!

These are facts!

TREASON – LETTER TO SENATOR "DICK" DURBIN

Senator Durbin,

I spent 27 years in the United States Air Force and flew three tours

in Vietnam. I consider it an honor and a privilege to have known
and served with so many great military men from the lowest ranks to
the highest in those years and since. The young men and women of
today are no less marvelous. I detested what Jane Fonda and John
Kerry did to our service men in that era, and I consider them both
traitors of almost the worst design. However, your largely fabricated
presentation on the Senate Floor of two days ago will ultimately
have worse effect upon this nation than what they did. You,
therefore have assumed the unheralded position of one of the worst
traitors I could ever imagine. Even Benedict Arnold had more
righteous reasons for treason than you have. You gave aid and
comfort to the enemy, you have abetted the terrorist by giving them
marvelous verbiage to scatter throughout the Muslim world. But,
worst of all, you have added to and altered a report which should
never have seen the light of day in a way that discredits the honor of
our fighting men today. You, sir, are now a man whom I shall loathe
far more than Fonda and Kerry. They made life miserable for our
POWs and got chicken blood spattered on our sacred uniforms as we
returned from the War. You, sir, have done your damnedest to
spatter the reputations and honor of these great warriors. Oh, don't
try to explain how esoteric your charges were and to now heap praise
upon our people. Your words are spread across the world now on Al
azerra and the Liberal media that wants to tear down America. You
attempted to disgrace every man and woman in the United States
Armed Services with your despicable, politically motivated weeping
session over the terrorist slime and scum that US Forces are holding
in Gitmo Bay. I will circulate what I have just written here as

widely as possible. I hope the pressure is so great upon you that you will have to resign in disgrace. You used our soldiers and Marines for your own personal political vendetta. Shameless and without honor, sir!

"The willingness with which our young people are likely to serve in any war, no matter how justified, shall be directly proportional as to how they perceive veterans of earlier wars and how they were treated and appreciated by this country."

GUESS WHO-MUST TRY TO GUESS

You really should be sitting down when you read this one.

Gold Star Mothers is an organization made up of women whose sons were killed in military combat during service in the United States armed forces.

Recently a delegation of New York State Gold Star Mothers made a trip to Washington, DC, to discuss various concerns with their elected representatives.

According to published reports, there was only one politician who refused to meet with these ladies.

Can you guess which politician that might be?

Was it New York Senator Charles Schumer? Nope, he met with them.

Try again.

Do you know anyone serving in the Senate who has never showed anything but contempt for our military?

Do you happen to know the name of any politician in Washington whose husband once wrote of his loathing for the military? Now you're getting warm! You got it!

None other than the Queen Bitch herself, Hillary Rotten Clinton. She refused repeated requests to meet with the Gold Star Mothers. Now, please don't tell me you're surprised. This woman wants to be President of the United States…and there is a huge percentage of voters who are eager to help her achieve that goal.

May you sleep in peace always...and please...hug or thank a Veteran for that privilege

Think about this one!

Don't forget, Queen Bitch Hillary Rodham Clinton, as a New York Senator, now comes under this fancy Congressional. It's common knowledge that, in order for her to establish NYS residency, they purchased a million+ dollar house in upscale Chappaqua, Makes sense.

Now, they are entitled to Secret Service protection for life.

Still makes sense.

Here is where it becomes interesting. The mortgage payments hover at about $10,000 per month. BUT, an extra residency had to be built within the acreage in order to house the Secret Service agents.

The Clinton's now charge the Secret Service $10,000 monthly rent for the use of said Secret Service residence and that rent is just about equal to their mortgage payment…meaning that we, the tax payers, are paying the Clinton's mortgage, their transportation, their safety and security, their 12 man staff, and it's all perfectly legal.

Please forward this to as many people as you can. We don't want this woman to even think of running for President. So, just how many people can you send this to? It will take no more than 2 minutes. Thanks

---

After hearing that the state of Florida changed its opinion and let a
Muslim woman have her picture on her driver's license with her face
covered, one American had had enough. This is an editorial written
by an American citizen, published in a Tampa newspaper. Did quite
a job, didn't he?

Immigrants, not Americans, must adapt.

I am tired of this nation worrying about whether we are offending
some individual or his culture. Since the terrorist attacks on Sept. 11,
we have experienced a surge in patriotism by the majority of
Americans. However, the dust from the attacks had barely settled
when the "politically correct" crowd began complaining about the
possibility that our patriotism was offending others. I am not against
immigration, nor do I hold a grudge against anyone who is seeking a
better life by coming to America. Our population is almost entirely
comprised of descendants of immigrants.

However, there are a few things that those who have recently come
to our country, and apparently some born here, need to understand.
This idea of America being a multicultural community has served
only to dilute our sovereignty and our national identity. As
Americans, we have. This culture has been developed over centuries
of struggles, trials, and victories by millions of men and women who
have sought freedom.

We speak English, not Spanish, Arabic, Chinese, Japanese, Russian,
or any other language. Therefore, if you wish to become part of our

society, learn the language! "In God We Trust" is our national motto. This is not some Christian, right-wing, political slogan. We adopted this motto because Christian men and women, on Christian principles, founded this nation, a fact which is abundantly documented. It is certainly appropriate to display it on the walls of our schools. If God offends you, then I suggest you consider another part of the world as your new home, because God is part of our culture.

If the Stars and Stripes offend you, or you don't like Uncle Sam, then you should seriously consider a move to another part of this planet. We are happy with our culture and have no desire to change, and we really don't care how you did things where you came from. This is our country, our land, and our lifestyle. Our First Amendment gives every citizen the right to express his opinion, and we will allow you every opportunity to do so.

But once you're done complaining, whining, and griping about our flag, our pledge, our national motto, or our way of life, I highly encourage you to take advantage of one other great American freedom: the right to leave!

If you agree, please pass this along.

RONALD REAGAN...THE MAN IN HIS OWN WORDS

1) "Here's my strategy on the Cold War: We win, they lose."

2) "The most terrifying words in the English language are: I'm from the government and I'm here to help."

3) "The trouble with our Liberal friends is not that they're ignorant: It's just that they know so much that isn't so."

4) "Of the four wars in my lifetime none came about because the U.S. was too strong."

5) "I have wondered at times about what the Ten Commandments would have looked like if Moses had run them through the U.S. Congress."

6) "The taxpayer: That's someone who works for the federal government but doesn't have to take the civil service examination."

7) "Government is like a baby: An alimentary canal with a big appetite at one end and no sense of responsibility at the other."

8) "If we ever forget that we're one nation under God, then we will be a nation gone under."

9) "The nearest thing to eternal life we will ever see on this earth is a government program."

10) "I've laid down the law, though, to everyone from now on about anything that happens: no matter what time it is, wake me, even if it's in the middle of a Cabinet meeting."

11) "It has been said that politics is the second oldest profession. I have learned that it bears a striking resemblance to the first."

12) "Government's view of the economy could be summed up in a few short phrases: If it moves, tax it. If it keeps moving, regulate it. And if it stops moving, subsidize it."

13) "Politics is not a bad profession. If you succeed there are many rewards, if you disgrace yourself you can always write a book."

14) "No arsenal, or no weapon in the arsenals of the world, is so formidable as the will and moral courage of free men and women.

Suppose you were an idiot. And suppose you were a member of Congress. But, I repeat myself.

--Mark Twain

We contend that for a nation to try to tax itself into prosperity is like a man standing in a bucket and trying to lift himself up by the handle.

--Winston Churchill

A government which robs Peter to pay Paul can always depend on the support of Paul.

--George Bernard Shaw

A Liberal is someone who feels a great debt to his fellow man, which
debt he proposes to pay off with your money.

-- G. Gordon Liddy

Democracy must be something more than two wolves and a sheep voting on what to have for dinner.

--James Bovard, Civil Libertarian (1994)

Foreign aid might be defined as a transfer from poor people in rich countries to rich people in poor countries.

--Douglas Casey, Classmate of W. J. Clinton at Georgetown U. (1992)

Giving money and power to government is like giving whiskey and car keys to teenage boys.

-- P.J. O'Rourke, Civil Libertarian

Government is the great fiction, through which everybody endeavors to live at the expense of everybody else.

-- Frederic Bastiat, French Economist (1801-1850)

I don't make jokes. I just watch the government and report the facts.

-- Will Rogers

If you think health care is expensive now, wait until you see what it costs when it's free.

-- P.J. O'Rourke

If you want government to intervene domestically, you're a Liberal. If you want government to intervene overseas, you're a Conservative. If you want government to intervene everywhere, you're a moderate. If you don't want government to intervene anywhere, you're an extremist.

-- Joseph Sobran, Editor of the National Review at one time (1995)

In general, the art of government consists in taking as much money as possible from one party of the citizens to give to the other.

-- Voltaire (1764)

Just because you do not take an interest in politics doesn't mean politics won't take an interest in you.

-- Pericles (430 B.C.)

No man's life, liberty, or property are safe while the legislature is in session.

-- Mark Twain (1866)

Talk is cheap-except when Congress does it. (Unknown)

The inherent vice of capitalism is the unequal sharing of the blessings. The inherent blessing of socialism is the equal sharing of misery.

-- Winston Churchill

The only difference between a tax man and a taxidermist is that the taxidermist leaves the skin.

-- Mark Twain

The ultimate result of shielding men from the effects of folly is to fill the world with fools.

-- Herbert Spencer, English Philosopher (1820-1903)

There is no distinctly native American criminal class save Congress.

-- Mark Twain

There is only one basic human right, the right to do as you damn well please. And with it comes the only basic human duty, the duty to take the consequences.

What this country needs are more unemployed politicians.

-- Edward Langley, Artist 1928-1995

When buying and selling are controlled by legislation, the first things to be bought and sold are legislators.

TO BE A DEMOCRAT, YOU HAVE TO BELIEVE THAT...

1) The AIDS virus is spread by a lack of funding.

2) Trial lawyers are selfless heroes and that doctors are overpaid.

3) Global temperatures are affected more by a suburban soccer mom driving an SUV than by documented, cyclical variations in the brightness and intensity of the sun.

4) Guns in the hands of law-abiding Americans are more of a threat than nuclear, chemical and biological weapons in the hands of Saddam Hussein.

5) Businesses create oppression and government creates prosperity.

6) Self-esteem is more important than doing anything to earn it.

7) There was no art before federal funding.

8) The NRA is a bad organization because it stands up for certain parts of the Constitution, but the ACLU is a good organization because it stands up for certain parts of the Constitution.

9) Taxes are too low but ATM fees are too high.

10) Standardized tests are racist, but racial quotas are not.

11) ANY change in the weather is proof of global warming.

12) National wealth is determine by what we consume, not by what we produce.

13) The only wars in which America should become involved are those in which our national security is not at risk.

14) Perjury and obstruction of justice are impeachable if a Republican president commits them but a harmless, private matter if a Democrat president commits them.

15) America can have a strong military without spending money on it.

16) The way to improve public school is to give more money and power to the very people who have misused that power and money to destroy the public schools.

17) Hunters and fishermen do not care about the environment but pasty-faced activists that rarely venture out-of-doors do.

18) A bureaucrat living in Washington, D.C. can make better decisions about how to spend the money that you earn than you can.

19) Being a movie or television star qualifies you to speak out on public policy.

20) Hillary Clinton is a wonderful example for young women of feminine independence even though she has never accomplished

anything worthwhile without riding on the coattails of her
husband.

21) A handful of religious whackos living in rural Texas are more of
a threat to public safety than Islamic terrorists who wish to plant
bombs in major American cities.

22) Passing new laws are a much better way to curb crime than
enforcing the existing ones.

23) Tax cuts are for people who don't actually pay income taxes.

WHAT IS A BILLION?

The next time you hear a politician use the word "billion," casually,
think about whether you want the politician spending your tax
money. A billion is a difficult number to comprehend, but one
advertising agency did a good job of putting that figure into
perspective in one of its releases.

1) A billion seconds ago it was 1959.

2) A billion minutes ago Jesus was alive.

3) A billion hours ago our ancestors were living in the Stone Age.

4) A billion days ago no-one walked on two feet on earth.

5) A billion dollars ago was only 8 hours and 20 minutes, at the rate
our government spends it.

While this thought is still fresh in our brain; let's take a look at New
Orleans. It's amazing what you can learn with some simple division.
Louisiana Senator, Mary Landrieu (D) is presently asking Congress
for 250-billion dollars to rebuild New Orleans. Interesting number;
what does it mean?

a) Well... if you are one of the 484,674 residents of New Orleans (every man, woman, and child) you <u>each</u> get $516,528

b) Or... if you have one of the 188,251 homes in New Orleans, your home gets $1,329,787

c) Or... if you are a family of four, your family gets $2,066,012

Washington, D.C.

HELLO!

Are all your calculators broken?

SO TRUE

Barack Obama meets with the Queen of England.

He asks her, "Your Majesty, how do you run such an efficient government? Are there any tips you can give to me?"

"Well," says the Queen, "the most important thing is to surround yourself with intelligent people."

Obama frowns "But how do I know the people around me are really intelligent?"

The Queen takes a sip of tea. "Oh, that's easy. You just ask them to answer an intelligent riddle."

The Queen pushes a button on her intercom. "Please send Tony Blair in here, would you?"

Tony Blair walks into the room. "Yes, my Queen?"

The Queen smiles; "Answer me this, please, Tony. Your mother and father have a child. It is not your brother and it is not your sister. Who is it?"

Without pausing for a moment, Tony Blair answers, "That would be me."

"Yes! Very good," says the Queen.

Obama goes back home to ask Joe Biden, his vice president, the same question.

"Joe. Answer this for me. Your mother and your father have a child. It's not your brother and it's not your sister. Who is it?" "I'm not sure," says Biden. "Let me get back to you on that one." He goes to his advisors and asks every one, but none can give him an answer. Finally, he ends up in the men's room and recognizes Colin Powell's shoes in the next stall.

Biden asks Powell, "Colin! Can you answer this for me? Your mother and father have a child and it's not your brother or your sister. Who is it?" Colin Powell yells back, "That's easy. It's me!" Biden smiles, and says, "Thanks!" Then, he goes back to speak with Obama.

"Say, I did some research and I have the answer to that riddle. It's Colin Powell."

Obama gets up, stomps over to Biden, and angrily yells into his face, "No, you idiot! It's Tony Blair!"

How Long Do We Have?

About the time our original thirteen states adopted their new constitution in 1787, Alexander Tyler, a Scottish history professor at the University of Edinburgh , had this to say about the fall of the Athenian Republic some 2,000 years earlier:

"A democracy is always temporary in nature; it simply cannot exist as a permanent form of government. A democracy will continue to exist up until the time that voters discover they can vote themselves generous gifts from the public treasury. From that moment on, the majority always vote for the candidates who promise the most benefits from the public treasury, with the result that every democracy will finally collapse due to loose fiscal policy, which is always followed by a dictatorship."

"The average age of the world's greatest civilizations from the beginning of history, has been about 200 years. During those 200 years, those nations always progressed through the following sequence:

1) From bondage to spiritual faith
2) From spiritual faith to great courage
3) From courage to liberty
4) From liberty to abundance
5) From abundance to complacency
6) From complacency to apathy
7) From apathy to dependence
8) From dependence back into bondage

Professor Joseph Olson of Hamline University School of Law, St. Paul, Minnesota, points out some interesting facts concerning the 2000 Presidential election:

Population of counties won by: Gore: 127 million; Bush: 143 million

Square miles of land won by: Gore: 580,000; Bush: 2,427,000

States won by: Gore: 19; Bush: 29

Murder rate per 100,000 residents in counties won by: Gore: 13.2; Bush: 2.1

Professor Olson adds:

"In aggregate, the map of the territory Bush won was mostly the land owned by the taxpaying citizens of this great country. Gore's territory mostly encompassed those citizens living in government-owned tenements and living off various forms of government welfare..."

Olson believes the United States is now somewhere between the "complacency and apathy" phase of Professor Tyler's definition of democracy, with some forty percent of the nation's population already having reached the "governmental dependency" phase.

If Congress grants amnesty and citizenship to twenty million criminal invaders called illegals and they vote, then goodbye to the USA in fewer than five years

---

In a news conference Deanna Favre announced she will be the starting QB for the Packers this coming Sunday. Deanna asserts that she is qualified to be starting QB because she has spent the past 16 years married to Brett while he played QB for the Packers. During this period of time she became familiar with the definition of a corner blitz, and is now completely comfortable with other terminology of the Packers offense. A survey of Packers fans shows that 50% of those polled supported the move.

Does this sound idiotic and unbelievable to you? Well, Hillary Clinton makes the same claims as to why she is qualified to be President and 50% of Democrats polled agreed. She has never run a City, County, or State.

When told Hillary Clinton has experience because she has 8 years in the white house, Dick Morris stated "so has the white house pastry chef".

BILL CLINTON'S MILITARY CAREER

For those who have forgotten, never knew or don't want to talk about it....Old draft evaders never die. They just have a haircut and shave. Scum of the earth!

1) Bill Clinton registers for the draft on September 08, 1964, accepting all contractual conditions of registering for the draft. Selective Service Number is 326 46 228.

2) Bill Clinton classified 2-S on November 17, 1964.

3) Bill Clinton reclassified 1-A on March 20, 1968.

4) Bill Clinton ordered to report for induction on July 28, 1969.

5) Bill Clinton refuses to report and is not inducted into the military.

6) Bill Clinton reclassified 1-D after enlisting in the United States

7) Army Reserves on August 07, 1969, under authority of COL. E. Holmes.

8) Clinton signs enlistment papers and takes oath of enlistment.

9) Bill Clinton fails to report to his duty station at the University of Arkansas ROTC, September 1969.

10) Bill Clinton reclassified 1-A on October 30, 1969, as enlistment with Army Reserves is revoked by Colonel E. Holmes and Clinton now AWOL and subject to arrest under Public Law 90-40 (2) (a) registrant who has failed to report...remain liable for induction.

11) Bill Clinton's birth date lottery number is 311, drawn December 1, 1969, but anyone who has already been ordered to report for induction is ineligible!

12) Bill Clinton runs for Congress (1974), while a fugitive from

justice under Public Law 90-40.

13) Bill Clinton runs for Arkansas Attorney General (1976), while a fugitive from justice.

14) Bill Clinton receives pardon on January 21, 1977, from President Carter.

15) Bill Clinton becomes the first pardoned federal felon ever to serve as President of the United States.

16) All these facts come from Freedom of Information requests, public laws, and various books that have been published, and have not been refuted by Clinton.

17) After the 1993 World Trade Center bombing, President Clinton promised that those responsible would be hunted down and punished.

18) After the 1995 bombing in Saudi Arabia, which killed five U.S. military personnel, Clinton promised that those responsible would be hunted down and punished.

19) After the 1996 Khobar Towers bombing in Saudi Arabia, which killed 19 and injured 200 U.S. military personnel, Clinton promised that those responsible would be hunted down and punished.

20) After the 1998 bombing of U.S. embassies in Africa, which killed 224 and injured 5,000, Clinton promised that those responsible would be hunted down and punished.

21) After the 2000 bombing of the USS Cole, which killed 17 and injured 39 U.S. sailors, Clinton promised that those responsible be hunted down and punished.

22) Maybe if Clinton had kept those promises, an estimated 3,000

people in New York and Washington, DC. who are now dead would be alive today.

Think about it! It is a strange turn of events. Hillary gets $8 Million for her forthcoming memoir. Bill gets about $12 Million for his memoir yet to be written. This from two people who spent 8 years being unable to recall anything about past events while under oath.

P.S. Please forward this to as many people as you can! We don't want this woman to even THINK of running for President

---

CONVENIENTLY FORGOTTEN FACTS

Back in 1969 a group of Black Panthers decided that a fellow black panther named Alex Rackley needed to die.

Rackley was suspected of disloyalty. Rackley was first tied to a chair. Once safely immobilized, his friends tortured him for hours by, among other things, pouring boiling water on him.

When they got tired of torturing Rackley, Black Panther member, Warren Kimbo took Rackley outside and put a bullet in his head.

Rackley's body was later found floating in a river about 25 miles north of New Haven, Connecticut.

Perhaps at this point you're curious as to what happened to these Black Panthers? In 1977, that's only eight years later, only one of the killers was still in jail.

The shooter, Warren Kimbro, managed to get a scholarship to Harvard and became good friends with none other than Al Gore. He later became an assistant dean at an Eastern Connecticut State College. Isn't that something?

As a '60s radical you can pump a bullet into someone's head and a few years later, in the same state, you can become an assistant college dean! Only in America!

Erica Huggins was the woman who served the Panthers by boiling the water for Mr. Rackley's torture.

Some years later Ms. Huggins was elected to a California School Board.

How in the world do you think these killers got off so easily?

Maybe it was in some part due to the efforts of two people who came to the defense of the Panthers. These two people actually went so far as to shut down Yale University with demonstrations in defense of the accused Black Panthers during their trial.

One of these people was none other than Bill Lan Lee. Mr. Lee, or Mr. Lan Lee, as the case may be, isn't a college dean. He isn't a member of a California School Board. He is now head of the United States Justice Department's Civil Rights Division, appointed by none other than Bill Clinton.

O.K., so who was the other Panther defender?

Is this other notable Panther defender now a school board member?

Is this other Panther apologist now an assistant college dean?

No, neither!

The other Panther defender was, like Lee, a radical law student at Yale University at the time. She is now known as The "smartest woman in the world."

She is none other than the Democratic senator from the State of New York - our former First Lady, the incredible Hillary Rodham Clinton.

And now, as Paul Harvey said; "You know the rest of the story".

Pass this on!

This deserves the widest possible press.

Also remember it, when, she runs for President.

NIGHTMARE OR DREAM? YOU DECIDE

Last night I had the strangest dream. It was so real, so life-like and so vivid I woke up in a cold sweat. Let me describe it to you briefly...

1) Hillary wins the Democratic Party nomination for President of the United States

2) Naturally, she wants to choose as her running mate someone with a lot of knowledge and experience in government and foreign affairs, someone who is a seasoned campaigner who could bring a lot of strength to the ticket. Who better than Bill, her husband?!

3) Hill and Bill go on to win the election in November and the Democrats maintain control of the House and the Senate.

4) Hillary is sworn in as President on January 20, 2009. The next day, after all the inauguration parties are over, she calls a press conference to make an announcement: she is resigning as President! Bill, as the Vice President, immediately becomes President!!! This is all perfectly legal under the 22nd Amendment to the Constitution; for it states that "no person may be elected as president more than twice". Bill is not being elected for a third term but is merely serving out the remainder of Hillary's term---all 4 years of it.

5) But wait! There's more! The following day Bill calls a press

conference to make an announcement. He has chosen someone to fill the now-vacant office of Vice President. Guess who he picks? Why, Hillary, of course!

Please forward this e-mail to all of your Republican friends and to as many others as you wish to cause sleepless nights

---

I'M CONFUSED

This was passed to me, but I can't understand it. Maybe you can. I'm trying to get all this political stuff straightened out in my head so I'll know how to vote come November. Right now, we have one guy saying one thing. Then the other guy says something else. Who to believe. Let me see; have I got this straight?

Clinton awards Halliburton no-bid contract in Yugoslavia - good...

Bush awards Halliburton no-bid contract in Iraq - bad...

Clinton spends 77 billion on war in Serbia - good...

Bush spends 87 billion in Iraq - bad...

Clinton imposes regime change in Serbia - good...

Bush imposes regime change in Iraq - bad...

Clinton bombs Christian Serbs on behalf of Muslim Albanian terrorists- good...

Bush liberates 25 million from a genocidal dictator - bad...

Clinton bombs Chinese embassy - good...

Bush bombs terrorist camps - bad...

Clinton commits felonies while in office - good...

Bush lands on aircraft carrier in jumpsuit - bad...

No mass graves found in Serbia - good...

No WMD found Iraq - bad...

Stock market crashes in 2000 under Clinton - good...

Economy on upswing under Bush - bad...

Clinton refuses to take custody of Bin Laden - good...

World Trade Center's fall under Bush - bad...

Clinton says Saddam has nukes - good...

Bush says Saddam has nukes - bad...

Clinton calls for regime change in Iraq - good...

Bush imposes regime change in Iraq - bad...

Terrorist training in Afghanistan under Clinton - good...

Bush destroys training camps in Afghanistan - bad...

Milosevic not yet convicted - good...

Saddam turned over for trial - bad...

It's so confusing!

Every year an independent tax watchdog group analyzes the average tax burden on Americans, and then calculates the "Tax Freedom Day". This is the day after which the money you earn goes to you, not the government. This year, tax freedom day was April 11th. That's the earliest it has been since 1991. Its latest day ever was May 2nd, which occurred in 2000. Notice anything special about those dates?

Recently, John Kerry gave a speech in which he claimed Americans are actually paying more taxes under Bush, despite the tax cuts. He gave no explanation and provided no data for this claim.

Another interesting fact: Both George Bush and John Kerry are wealthy men.

Bush owns only one home, his ranch in Texas. Kerry owns 4 mansions, all worth several million dollars. (His ski resort home in

Idaho is an old barn brought over from Europe in pieces. Not your average A-frame).

Bush paid $250,000 in taxes this year; Kerry paid $90,000. Does that sound right? The man who wants to raise your taxes obviously has figured out a way to avoid paying his own.

ANT & GRASSHOPPER REVISITED

Old version:

The ant works hard in the withering heat all summer long, building his house and laying up supplies for the winter. The grasshopper thinks he's a fool and laughs and dances and plays the summer away. Come winter, the ant is warm and well fed. The grasshopper has no food or shelter so he dies out in the cold.

Moral of the story: be responsible for yourself!

Modern version:

The ant works hard in the withering heat all summer long, building his house and laying up supplies for the winter. The grasshopper thinks he's a fool and laughs and dances and plays the summer away. Come winter, the shivering grasshopper calls a press conference and demands to know why the ant should be allowed to be warm and well fed while others are cold and starving.

CBS, NBC, ABC, CNN and all the other "left wing media" groups show up to provide pictures of the shivering grasshopper next to a video of the ant in his comfortable home with a table filled with food. America is stunned by the sharp contrast. How can this be, that in a country of such wealth, this poor grasshopper is allowed to suffer so?

Kermit the Frog appears on Oprah with the grasshopper, and everybody cries when they sing "It's Not Easy Being Green." Jesse Jackson stages a demonstration in front of the ant's house where the news stations film the group singing "We shall overcome." Jesse then has the group kneel down to pray to God for the grasshopper's sake.

Tom Daschle and Nancy Pelosi exclaim in an interview with Peter Jennings that the ant has gotten rich off the back of the grasshopper, and both call for an immediate tax hike on the ant to make him pay his "fair share."

Finally, the EEOC drafts the "Economic Equity and Anti-Grasshopper Act," retroactive to the beginning of the summer.

The ant is fined for failing to hire a proportionate number of green bugs and, having nothing left to pay his retroactive taxes, his home is confiscated by the government.

Hillary represents the grasshopper in a defamation suit against the ant and the case is tried before a panel of federal judges that Bill appointed from a list of single-parent welfare recipients.

The ant loses the case.

The story ends as we see the grasshopper finishing up the last bits of the ant's food while the government house he lives in, which just happens to be the ant's old house, crumbles around him because he doesn't maintain it.

The ant has disappeared in the snow.

The grasshopper is found dead in a drug related incident and the house, now abandoned, is taken over by a gang of spiders who terrorize the once peaceful neighborhood.

Moral of the story: Vote Republican

IF IT WERE JUST THIS SIMPLE

Zell Miller knows how to boil things down to the basics. That's what Georgia's junior senator did Thursday when he explained why it's important that Saddam Hussein be defanged. But he's also a good storyteller. Here's the text of Mr. Miller's remarks, made on the Senate floor about the need to help President Bush deal with Iraq. We couldn't say it any better.

"Mr. President, I have signed on as an original co-sponsor of the Iraq resolution, and I'd like to tell you a story about why I think it is the right path to take: A few weeks ago, we were doing some work on my back porch back home, tearing out a section of old stacked rocks, when all of a sudden I uncovered a nest of copperhead snakes. Now, I'm not one to get alarmed at snakes. I know they perform some useful functions, like eating rats. And when I was a young lad, I kept snakes as pets. I had an indigo snake, a bull snake, a corn snake and many others. I must have had a dozen king snakes at one time or another. They make great pets and you only had to feed them a mouse every 30 days.

I read all the books by Raymond C. Ditmars, who was the foremost herpetologist of his day. That's an expert on snakes. For a while, I wanted to be a herpetologist, but the pull of being a big-league shortstop outran that childhood dream. I reminisce this way to explain that snakes don't scare me like they do some people. And I guess the reason is that I know the difference between those that are harmless and those that will kill you. In fact, I bet I may be the only

147

senator in this body who can look at the last three inches of a snake's tail and tell you whether it's poisonous or not. I can also tell the sex of a snake, but that's another story.

A copperhead will kill you. It could kill one of my dogs. It could kill one of my grandchildren. It could kill any of my four great grandchildren. They play all the time where I found these killers. And you know, when I discovered these copperheads, I didn't call my wife Shirley and ask her advice, like I do on most things. I didn't yell for help from my neighbors or take it to the city council. I just took a hoe and knocked them in the head and killed them dead as a doorknob.

I guess you could call it a unilateral action, or pre-emptive or even bellicose and reactive. I took their poisonous heads off because they were a threat to me. And they were a threat to my home and my family. They were a threat to all I hold dear.

And isn't that what this is all about?"

$64,000 QUESTION ASKED…

Shades of Orwell's 1984, all animals are equal, but pigs are more equal than others. It's time to clean house folks. I can't think of ONE incumbent that needs to return to Washington.

Recently on ABC (better known as the "all-barrack channel"), during the "network special on health care", Obama was asked: "Mr. president will you and your family give up your current health care program and join the new 'universal health care program' that the rest of us will be on ????"… (Bet you already know the answer)...

There was a stony silence as Obama ignored the question and chose not to answer it...

In addition, a number of Senators were asked the same question and their response was..."we will think about it." And they did. It was announced that the "Kennedy health care bill" was written into the new health care reform initiative, ensuring that that Congress will be 100% exempt! They have about 10 options, all administered by the private sector. This should speak volumes to all of us.

So, this great new health care plan that is good for you and me is not good enough for Obama, his family or Congress? We (the American public) need to stop this proposed debacle asap!

If you agree please pass this on…if not, plan to suffer with the Obama health care plan…for free…while our self-serving politicians make sure that they take care of themselves and their families at our expense. Remember – they are your servants --- you are not their servants!

'Am I the only guy in this country who's fed up with what's happening? Where the hell is our outrage? We should be screaming bloody murder! We've got a gang of clueless bozos steering our ship of state right over a cliff, we've got corporate gangsters stealing us blind, and we can't even clean up after a hurricane much less build a hybrid car. But instead of getting mad, everyone sits around and nods their heads when the politicians say, 'Stay the course…'

Stay the course? You've got to be kidding. This is America, not the damned, 'Titanic'. I'll give you a sound bite: 'Throw all the bums out!'

You might think I'm getting senile, that I've gone off my rocker, and maybe I have... But someone has to speak up. I hardly recognize this country anymore...

The most famous business leaders are not the innovators but the guys in handcuffs... While we're fiddling in Iraq, the Middle East is burning and nobody seems to know what to do. And the press is waving 'pom-poms' instead of asking hard questions. That's not the promise of the ' America ' my parents and yours traveled across the ocean for. I've had enough. How about you?

I'll go a step further. You can't call yourself a patriot if you're not outraged. This is a fight I'm ready and willing to have. The Biggest 'C' is Crisis! (Iacocca elaborates on nine C's of leadership, with crisis being the first.)

Leaders are made, not born. Leadership is forged in times of crisis. It's easy to sit there with your feet up on the desk and talk theory. Or send someone else's kids off to war when you've never seen a battlefield yourself. It's another thing to lead when your world comes tumbling down.

On September 11, 2001, we needed a strong leader more than any other time in our history. We needed a steady hand to guide us out of the ashes. A hell of a mess, so here's where we stand.

We're immersed in a bloody war with no plan for winning and no plan for leaving.

We're running the biggest deficit in the history of the country.

We're losing the manufacturing edge to Asia, while our once-great companies are getting slaughtered by health care costs.

Gas prices are skyrocketing, and nobody in power has a coherent energy policy. Our schools are in trouble.

Our borders are like sieves.

The middle class is being squeezed every which way.

These are times that cry out for leadership.

But when you look around, you've got to ask: 'Where have all the leaders gone?' Where are the curious, creative communicators? Where are the people of character, courage, conviction, omnipotence, and common sense? I may be a sucker for alliteration, but I think you get the point.

Name me a leader who has a better idea for homeland security than making us take off our shoes in airports and throw away our shampoo?

We've spent billions of dollars building a huge new bureaucracy, and all we know how to do is react to things that have already happened. Name me one leader who emerged from the crisis of Hurricane Katrina. Congress has yet to spend a single day evaluating the response to the hurricane or demanding accountability for the decisions that were made in the crucial hours after the storm. Everyone's hunkering down, fingers crossed, hoping it doesn't happen again. Now, that's just crazy. Storms happen. Deal with it. Make a plan. Figure out what you're going to do the next time.

Name me an industry leader who is thinking creatively about how we can restore our competitive edge in manufacturing. Who would have believed that there could ever be a time when 'The Big Three' referred to Japanese car companies? How did this happen, and more important, what are we going to do about it?

Name me a government leader who can articulate a plan for paying down the debit, or solving the energy crisis, or managing the health care problem. The silence is deafening. But these are the crises that are eating away at our country and milking the middle class dry.

I have news for the gang in Congress. We didn't elect you to sit on your asses and do nothing and remain silent while our democracy is being hijacked and our greatness is being replaced with mediocrity. What is everybody so afraid of? That some bonehead on NBC news or CNN news will call them a name? Give me a break. Why don't you guys show some spine for a change?

Had Enough? Hey, I'm not trying to be the voice of gloom and doom here. I'm trying to light a fire. I'm speaking out because I have hope - I believe in America... In my lifetime, I've had the privilege of living through some of America's greatest moments. I've also experienced some of our worst crises: The 'Great Depression,' 'World War II,' the 'Korean War,' the 'Kennedy Assassination,' the 'Vietnam War,' the 1970's oil crisis, and the struggles of recent years culminating with 9/11.

If I've learned one thing, it's this: 'you don't get anywhere by standing on the sidelines waiting for somebody else to take action. Whether it's building a better car or building a better future for our children, we all have a role to play. That's the challenge I'm raising in this book. It's a "Call to Action" for people who, like me, believe in America '. It's not too late, but it's getting pretty close. So let's shake off the crap and go to work. Let's tell 'em all we've had 'enough.'

Make your own contribution by sending this to everyone you know and care about. It's our country, folks, and it's our future. Our future is at stake!!

ANGRY ABOUT CONGRESS? READ 545 VERSUS 300,000,000...INTERESTING

Here it is again, heed or bleed. Politicians could care less about you except when it's time to vote. 1/3 of the Senate and all of Congress are up for vote in 2010--get the phonies out and clamor for term limits for these useless employees you hired!

Keep this one going till next elections are done. it may be our only hope.

We need to vote out all 545 and start all over. This email should be passed on all over the USA. Elections start next year, let us get them out!

545 versus 300,000,000

Every citizen needs to read this and think about what this journalist has scripted in this message. read it and then really think about our current political debacle.

Politicians are the only people in the world who create problems and then campaign against them.

Have you ever wondered, if both the Democrats and the Republicans are against deficits, why do we have deficits?

Have you ever wondered, if all the politicians are against inflation and high taxes, why do we have inflation and high taxes?

You and I don't propose a federal budget.

The president does.

You and I don't have the Constitutional authority to vote on appropriations.

The House of Representatives does. You and I don't write the tax code, Congress does.

153

You and I don't set fiscal policy, Congress does.

You and I don't control monetary policy, the Federal Reserve Bank does.

One hundred Senators, 435 Congressmen, one president, and nine Supreme Court justices equates to 545 human beings out of the 300 million are directly, legally, morally, and individually responsible for the domestic problems that plague this country.

I excluded the members of the Federal Reserve Board because that problem was created by the Congress. In 1913, Congress delegated its Constitutional duty to provide a sound currency to a federally chartered, but private, central bank.

I excluded all the special interests and lobbyists for a sound reason. They have no legal authority. They have no ability to coerce a senator, a Congressman, or a president to do one cotton-picking thing. I don't care if they offer a politician $1 million dollars in cash. The politician has the power to accept or reject it. No matter what the lobbyist promises, it is the legislator's responsibility to determine how he votes.

Those 545 human beings spend much of their energy convincing you that what they did is not their fault. They cooperate in this common con regardless of party. What separates a politician from a normal human being is an excessive amount of gall. No normal human being would have the gall of a Speaker, who stood up and criticized the President for creating deficits. The president can only propose a budget. He cannot force the Congress to accept it. The Constitution, which is the supreme law of the land, gives sole responsibility to the House of Representatives for originating and approving appropriations and taxes. Who is the speaker of the House? Nancy Pelosi. She is the leader of the majority party. She and fellow House members, not the president, can approve any budget they want. If the president vetoes it, they can pass it over his veto if they agree to.

It seems inconceivable to me that a nation of 300 million cannot replace 545 people who stand convicted -- by present facts -- of incompetence and irresponsibility. I can't think of a single domestic problem that is not traceable directly to those 545 people. When you fully grasp the plain truth that 545 people exercise the power of the federal government, then it must follow that what exists is what they want to exist.

If the tax code is unfair, it's because they want it unfair.

If the budget is in the red, it's because they want it in the red.

If the Army & Marines are in IRAQ , it's because they want them in IRAQ.

If they do not receive social security but are on an elite retirement plan not available to the people, it's because they want it that way. There are no insoluble government problems.

Do not let these 545 people shift the blame to bureaucrats, whom they hire and whose jobs they can abolish; to lobbyists, whose gifts and advice they can reject; to regulators, to whom they give the power to regulate and from whom they can take this power. Above all, do not let them con you into the belief that there exists disembodied mystical forces like "the economy," "inflation," or "politics" that prevent them from doing what they take an oath to do. Those 545 people, and they alone, are responsible.

They, and they alone, have the power.

They, and they alone, should be held accountable by the people who are their bosses.

Provided the voters have the gumption to manage their own employees.

We should vote all of them out of office and clean up their mess!

What you do with this article now that you have read it...Is up to you.

WE REMEMBER SEPTEMBER 11, 2001

President George W. Bush holding the badge of a police officer killed in the September 11, 2001 attacks.

"And I will carry this. It is the police shield of a man named George Howard, who died at the World Trade Center trying to save others. It was given to me by his mom, Arlene, as a proud memorial to her son. This is my reminder of lives that ended, and a task that does not end."

President Bush in his address to Congress September 20, 2001

INTERESTING INFO...

This is so neat...

Obama didn't think going to FT Hood TX was important enough, but guess who did?!

What a heartwarming story

Ft. Hood, TX

Just got this email from a trusted friend in San Antonio

In Dothan, AL a man had a TV on in his office when the news of the military base shootings came on. The husband of one of his employees was stationed there.

He called her into his office and the minute he told her what was going on, she got a text message from her husband saying, "I am okay." The cell phone started ringing right after that. It was an ER nurse. She said, "I'm the one who just sent you a text, not your husband." She thought the message would be comforting, but she immediately knew she had to let the wife know what was going on. She said, "I am sorry but your husband has been shot 4 times and he is in surgery."

The wife left Dothan and drove all night.

Miraculously, here is the photo I just received from my friend that was taken today in the hospital room. He is awake and will recover. His wife, who lives in Dothan, made it to Ft. Hood about the time he was waking up. Thought I'd share this great outcome.

Now this is what a President should do:

Did you see this in the media?

REPLY FROM MY CONGRESSMAN PHIL GINGREY

Thank you for contacting me regarding the Economic Stimulus Package. As your Congressman, I appreciate hearing your thoughts and welcome every opportunity to be of service.

As you may be aware, President Obama requested an almost one trillion dollar stimulus package in January. On January 26, 2009, Representative David Obey of Wisconsin introduced H.R. 1, the American Recovery and Reinvestment Act of 2009. This legislation initially passed the House of Representatives by a vote of 244 to 188 on January 28 and passed the Senate-with changes-by a vote of 61 to 37 on February 10, 2009.

On February 13, 2009, a compromise agreement totaling $787 billion passed both the House and the Senate. President Obama signed the bill into law on February 17, 2009. After careful consideration, I voted against both the initial House version and the final compromise.

While there is no doubt that our economy faces significant challenges, I earnestly do not believe this stimulus package is the right way to overcome these challenges. Over the past six months, Americans have watched as trillions and trillions of dollars of taxpayer dollars have been thrown at the economy through loans and government spending-with little positive effect.

The only way to truly stimulate the economy is to put taxpayer dollars back into the hands of the taxpayers. For this reason, I cosponsored H.R. 470, the Economic Recovery and Middle Class Tax Relief Act. This bill would provide an across the board income tax cut of 5%, repeal the Alternative Minimum Tax, increase the child tax credit, cut the top corporate tax rate, and make the Research and Development tax credit permanent.

Unlike the stimulus plan, H.R. 470 would also save money through a 1% across the board cut to all non-defense federal discretionary spending. It would create twice as many jobs as the stimulus bill at half of the cost. I will continue to stand up for commonsense, pro-growth solutions to strengthen our economy without leaving trillions and trillions of dollars in debt to future generations.

Again, thank you for sharing your concerns. If you feel that I may be of additional assistance on this, or any other matter of importance to you, please do not hesitate to contact me. I also invite you to sign up for my weekly email newsletter, or to share your ideas and opinions.

CHRISTMAS FOR THE ACLU

Pass this on to your church, co-workers, family, and friends.

What do you have to lose but 44 cents, what you have to gain more than you will ever know.

What a clever idea! Yes, Christmas cards. This is coming early so that you can get ready to include an important address to your list.

Want to have some fun this Christmas? Send the ACLU a Christmas card this year.

As they are working so very hard to get rid of the Christmas part of this holiday, we should all send them a nice, Christian card to brighten up their dark, sad, little world...

Make sure it says "Merry Christmas" on it.

Here's the address, just don't be rude or crude. (It's not the Christian way, you know.)

ACLU

125 Broad Street

18th Floor

New York , NY 10004

Two tons of Christmas cards would freeze their operations because they wouldn't know if any were regular mail containing contributions. So spend 44 cents and tell the ACLU to leave Christmas alone. Also tell them that there is no such thing as a "Holiday Tree". It's always been called a Christmas tree!

And pass this on to your email lists. We really want to communicate with the ACLU! They really deserve us!!

For those of you who aren't aware of them, the ACLU, (the American Civil Liberties Union) is the one suing the U.S. Government to take God, Christmas or anything Christian away from us. They represent the atheists and others in this war. Help put Christ back in Christmas!

ELECTIONS 2010/2012

All I ask is that you consider the suggestion here.

I realize that a few Members of each House are trustworthy, but, they don't stand and fight to stop bad legislation. As a group they are absolutely the most corrupt bunch to ever disgrace our Nation. In November of 2010 the entire House of Representatives will stand for re-election; all 435 of them. One third of the Senate, a total of 33 of them, will also stand for re-election. Vote every incumbent out. And I mean every one of them. No matter their Party affiliation. Let's start all over in the House of Representatives with 435 people who have absolutely no experience in running that body, with no political favors owed to anyone but their own constituents. Let's make them understand that they work for us. They are answerable to us and they simply have to run that body with some common sense. Two years later, in 2012, vote the next third of the incumbents in the Senate out.

We can do the same thing in 2014 and, by that time we will have put all new people in that body as well.

We, the People, have got to take this Country back and we have to do it peacefully.

That's what the Framers of our Constitution envisioned.

I am also suggesting term limits on the new bunch: 8 years for Representatives and 12 years for Senators – no exceptions. The longer they stay in office, the more power they get, and they love it and will do anything to get re-elected.

We have term-limited the President, now let's term-limit the Legislators.

Please, if you love this Country, send this (as I have done) to absolutely everyone whose email address appears in your address book.

This thing can permeate this Country in no time. Let's make it happen.

Don't just delete this - please pass it on and give our Country a fighting chance.

Vote the power abusers out....let's take America back!

If you like the way things are going in our country, and then do nothing...

THE PROPOSAL

When a company falls on difficult times, one of the things that seems to happen is they reduce their staff and workers. The remaining workers must find ways to continue to do a good job or risk that their job would be eliminated as well.

Wall Street, and the media normally congratulate the CEO for making this type of "tough decision," and his board of directors gives him a big bonus.

Our government should not be immune from similar risks.

Therefore:

Reduce the House of Representatives from the current 435 members to 218 members.

Reduce Senate members from 100 to 50 (one per State). Then, reduce their staff by 25%.

Accomplish this over the next 8 years (two steps/two elections) and of course this would require some redistricting.

Some Yearly Monetary Gains Include:

$44,108,400 for elimination of base pay for Congress (267 members X $165,200 pay/member/ year)

$97,175,000 for elimination of their staff (estimate $1.3 Million in staff per each member of the House, and $3 Million in staff per each member of the Senate every year)

$240,294 for the reduction in remaining staff by 25%

$7,500,000,000 reduction in pork barrel ear-marks each year (those members whose jobs are gone (current estimates for total government pork earmarks are at $15 Billion/year).

The remaining representatives would need to work smarter and improve efficiencies. It might even be in their best interests to work together for the good of our country!

We may also expect that smaller committees might lead to a more efficient resolution of issues as well... It might even be easier to keep track of what your representative is doing.

Congress has more tools available to do their jobs than it had back in 1911 when the current number of representatives was established (telephone, computers, cell phones to name a few)

Note:

Congress did not hesitate to head home when it was a holiday, when the nation needed a real fix to the economic problems. Also, we had 3 Senators that were not doing their jobs for the 18+ months (on the campaign trail) and still they all have accepted full pay. These facts alone support a reduction in Senators & Congress.

Summary of opportunity:

$ 44,108,400 reduction of Congress members

$282,100, 000 for elimination of the reduced house member staff

$150,000,000 for elimination of reduced Senate member staff

$59,675,000 for 25% reduction of staff for remaining house members

$37,500,000 for 25% reduction of staff for remaining Senate members

$7,500,000,000 reduction in pork added to bills by the reduction of Congress members

$8,073,383,400 per year estimated total savings (that's 8-BILLION just to start!)

Big business does these types of cuts all the time.

If Congresspersons were required to serve 20, 25 or 30 years (like everyone else) in order to collect retirement benefits, tax payers could save a bundle.

Now they get full retirement after serving only ONE term.

IF you are happy with how Congress spends our taxes, delete this message. Otherwise, I assume you know what to do.

OBAMA CAN'T BE BOTHERED BY ISLAMIC TERRORISM

In the wake of the terrorist strike on our soldiers at Fort Hood, one individual's still missing in action: Our commander in chief. The massacre's 51 casualties, including 13 dead, were insufficient to drag President Obama away from the White House Happy Hour. We just saw the worst terror attack on America since 9/11. And Obama couldn't adjust his schedule to support our grieving troops. Instead, we got his subtle defense of the perp: Unwilling to use the word "terror," let alone the phrase "Islamist terror," Obama warned us not to "rush to judgment."

A Muslim fanatic, known to the FBI as a fan of suicide bombers and to colleagues as an opponent of our government, coolly buys weapons, heads to a military facility he knows will be packed with unsuspecting soldiers, waits for the crowd to thicken, then shouts, "Allah is great!" and guns down 51 patriots, calmly reloading among the dead and dying.

But don't rush to judgment.

Imagine if, instead of Fort Hood, the massacre had gone down at a mosque in Detroit — carried out by a maddened Christian or Jew. Obama would've been aboard Air Force One before the pilots had time to file a flight plan and he would've been on site before the gun smoke cleared, hugging and boo-hooing and dispensing stirring rhetoric for the evening news.

But go out of his way to rally our butchered troops? Not a chance. It's not like they're real human beings with Ivy League degrees. When Obama got word of the attack, he didn't even lose his fabled cool.

Obama may be shamed into visiting Ft. Hood at some point, but his priority since Thursday has remained socializing American medicine. What happens in Texas stays in Texas.

Move on? Yes we can!

Of course, this act of Islamist terrorism has been an inconvenience to a president whose administration insists there's no such thing. Those dead and wounded soldiers are such an embarrassment. If only a Baptist or Lutheran had been the shooter, things would've been so much tidier.

What's next? The White House is going to bring heavy pressure on the FBI, through Attorney General Eric Holder, to play down investigative results confirming that Maj. Nidal Hasan was motivated by his Muslim beliefs.

Instead, we'll hear even more about the "harassment" Hasan suffered as the media toe the line laid down by the vile lead editorial in Saturday's New York Times and how this calculating terrorist contracted PTSD from his patients.

Let me kill the harassment myth right now: Political correctness rules in today's Army. We even protect our enemies these days. Had any soldier harassed Hasan because of his Islamist nuttiness, that soldier would've disappeared faster than a Franklin on a Times Square sidewalk.

Any snarky remarks directed toward Hasan — if there were any — would've come in reaction to his railing against our government, our military's mission and the monstrous injustice that, after grabbing an education in psychiatry worth hundreds of thousands of dollars from our military, he might have had to do his duty.

Far from being harassed himself, this creep was allowed to harass the soldiers he treated for stress disorders. According to colleagues, Hasan not only argued with his patients about our wars, but preached Islam to those under his care. (Just what troubled vets needed, no doubt?)

Prejudice? You bet. In this terrorist's favor. Nobody in Hasan's chain of command had the sense of duty to weed this pervert out. Why? Hasan would've accused them of discrimination. And the officer who brought charges against Hasan would've been the one whose career suffered.

Since writing on this travesty in the Post and speaking out on Fox News, I've been deluged with supportive messages — many from soldiers outraged at the politically correct treatment of this terrorist by the media, by senior military leaders — and by the president.

How many more Americans have to die, at home and in war, before our president admits that there is, indeed, such a thing as Islamist terror? Will he ever admit that it played a role in the tragedy at Fort Hood?

Not a chance. Islam's a religion of peace. America's the problem. And don't you forget it.

LETTER TO BARBARA BOXER

Excellent letter…wish more people in this country would speak their mind.

Some of us witnessed the arrogance of Barbara Boxer (D-CA) as she admonished a brigadier general because he addressed her as "ma'am" and not "Senator" before a Senate hearing. This letter is from a National Guard aviator and Captain for Alaska Airlines. I wonder what he would have said if he were really angry.

Long fly Alaska!

You were so right on when you scolded the general on TV for using the term, "ma'am," instead of "Senator". After all, in the military, "ma'am" is a term of respect when addressing a female of superior rank or position. The general was totally wrong...you are not a person of superior rank or position. You are a member of one of the world's most corrupt organizations, the U.S. Senate, equaled only by the U.S. House of Representatives.

Congress is a cesspool of liars, thieves, inside traders, traitors, drunks (one who killed a staffer, yet is still revered), criminals, and other low level swine who, as individuals (not all, but many), will do anything to enhance their lives, fortunes and power, all at the expense of the People of the United States and its Constitution, in order to be continually re-elected. Many Democrats even want American troops killed by releasing photographs. How many of you could honestly say, "We pledge our lives, our fortunes and our sacred honor"? None? One? Two?

Your reaction to the general shows several things. First is your abysmal ignorance of all things military. Your treatment of the general shows you to be an elitist of the worst kind. When the general entered the military (as most of us who served) he wrote the government a blank check, offering his life to protect your derriere, now safely and comfortably ensconced in a 20 thousand dollar leather chair, paid for by the general's taxes. You repaid him for this by humiliating him in front of millions.

Second is your puerile character, lack of sophistication, and arrogance which borders on the hubristic. This display of brattish behavior shows you to be a virago, termagant, harridan, nag, scold or shrew, unfit for your position, regardless of the support of the unwashed, uneducated masses that have made California into the laughing stock of the nation.

What I am writing, Senator, are the same thoughts countless millions of Americans have toward Congress, but who lack the energy, ability or time to convey them. Under the Democrats, some don't even have the 44 cents to buy the stamp. Regardless of their thoughts, most realize that politicians are pretty much the same, and will vote for the one who will bring home the most bacon, even if they do consider how corrupt that person is. Lord Acton (1834 - 1902) so aptly charged, "Power tends to corrupt and absolute power corrupts absolutely." Unbeknownst to you and your colleagues, "Mr. Power" has had his way with all of you, and we are all the worse for it.

Finally Senator, I, too, have a title. It is "Right Wing Extremist Potential Terrorist Threat."

It is not of my choosing, but was given to me by your Secretary of Homeland Security, Janet Napolitano. And you were offended by "ma'am"?

Have a fine day. Cheers!

CASH FOR CODGERS

Just in...

Democrats, realizing the success of the President's "Cash for Clunkers" rebate program, have revamped a major portion of their National Health Care Plan.

President Obama, Speaker Pelosi, and Sen. Reed are expected to make this major announcement at a joint news conference later this week. I have obtained an advanced copy of the proposal which is named..."cash for codgers": and it works like this... Couples wishing to access health care funds in order to pay for the delivery of a child will be required to turn in one old person.

The amount the government grants them will be fixed according to a sliding scale. Older and more prescription dependent codgers will garner the highest amounts.

Special "Bonuses" will be paid for those submitting codgers in targeted groups, such as smokers, alcohol drinkers, persons 10 pounds over their government prescribed weight, and any member of the Republican Party.

Smaller bonuses will be given for codgers who consume beef, soda, fried foods, potato chips, lattes, whole milk, dairy products, bacon, Brussels sprouts, or Girl Scout Cookies.

All codgers will be rendered totally useless via toxic injection. This will insure that they are not secretly resold or their body parts harvested to keep other codgers in repair.

Run, seniors, run!

A MUST READ

Juval Aviv was the Israeli Agent upon whom the movie ' Munich ' was based. He was Golda Meir's bodyguard -- she appointed him to track down and bring to justice the Palestinian terrorists who took the Israeli athletes hostage and killed them during the Munich Olympic Games.

In a lecture in New York City a few weeks ago, he shared information that every American needs to know -- but that our government has not yet shared with us.

He predicted the London subway bombing on the Bill O'Reilly show on Fox News stating publicly that it would happen within a week. At the time, O'Reilly laughed and mocked him saying that in a week he wanted him back on the show. But, unfortunately, within a week the terrorist attack had occurred.

Juval Aviv gave intelligence (via what he had gathered in Israel and the Middle East) to the Bush Administration about 9/11 a month before it occurred. His report specifically said they would use planes as bombs and target high profile buildings and monuments. Congress has since hired him as a security consultant. Now for his future predictions:

He predicts the next terrorist attack on the U.S. will occur within the next few months.

Forget hijacking airplanes, because he says terrorists will never try and hijack a plane again as they know the 20 people onboard will never go down quietly again. Aviv believes our airport security is a joke -- that we have been reactionary rather than proactive in developing strategies that are truly effective.

For example:

Our airport technology is outdated. We look for metal, and the new explosives are made of plastic.

He talked about how some idiot tried to light his shoe on fire. Because of that, now everyone has to take off their shoes. A group of idiots tried to bring aboard liquid explosives. Now we can't bring liquids on board. He says he's waiting for some suicidal maniac to pour liquid explosive on his underwear; at which point, security will have us all traveling naked! Every strategy we have is reactionary. We only focus on security when people are heading to the gates. Aviv says that if a terrorist attack targets airports in the future, they will target busy times on the front end of the airport when/where people are checking in. It would be easy for someone to take two suitcases of explosives, walk up to a busy check-in line, ask a person next to them to watch their bags for a minute while they run to the restroom or get a Drink, and then detonate the bags before security even gets involved.

In Israel, security checks bags before people can even enter the airport.

Aviv says the next terrorist attack here in America is imminent and will involve suicide bombers and non-suicide bombers in places where large groups of people congregate. (I. E., Disneyland, Las Vegas casinos, big cities (New York, San Francisco, Chicago, etc..) and that it will also include shopping malls, subways in rush hour, train stations, etc., as well as rural America this time (Wyoming, Montana, etc.).

The attack will be characterized by simultaneous detonations around the country (terrorists like big impact), involving at least 5-8 cities, including rural areas.

Aviv says terrorists won't need to use suicide bombers in many of the larger cities, because at places like the MGM Grand in Las Vegas, they can simply valet park a car loaded with explosives and walk away.

Aviv says all of the above is well known in intelligence circles, but that our U. S. Government does not want to 'alarm American citizens' with the facts. The world is quickly going to become 'a different place', and issues like 'global warming' and political correctness will become totally irrelevant.

On an encouraging note, he says that Americans don't have to be concerned about being nuked. Aviv says the terrorists who want to destroy America will not use sophisticated weapons. They like to use suicide as a front-line approach. It's cheap, it's easy, it's effective; and they have an infinite abundance of young militants more than willing to 'meet their destiny'.

He also says the next level of terrorists, over which America should be most concerned, will not be coming from abroad. But will be, instead, 'homegrown' -- having attended and been educated in our own schools and universities right here in the U. S. He says to look for 'students' who frequently travel back and forth to the Middle East..These young terrorists will be most dangerous because they will know our language and will fully understand the habits of Americans; but that we Americans won't know/understand a thing about them.

Aviv says that, as a people, Americans are unaware and uneducated about the terrorist threats we will, inevitably, face. America still has only have a handful of Arabic and Farsi speaking people in our intelligence networks, and Aviv says it is critical that we change that fact SOON.

So, what can America do to protect itself? From an intelligence perspective, Aviv says the U.S. needs to stop relying on satellites and technology for intelligence. We need to, instead, follow Israel's, Ireland's and England's hands-on examples of human intelligence, both from an infiltration perspective as well as to trust 'aware' citizens to help. We need to engage and educate ourselves as citizens; however, our U. S. government continues to treat us, its citizens, 'like babies'. Our government thinks we 'can't handle the truth' and are concerned that we'll panic if we understand the realities of terrorism. Aviv says this is a deadly mistake.

Aviv recently created/executed a security test for our Congress, by placing an empty briefcase in five well-traveled spots in five major cities. The results? Not one person called 911 or sought a policeman to check it out. In fact, in Chicago, someone tried to steal the briefcase!

In comparison, Aviv says that citizens of Israel are so well 'trained' that an unattended bag or package would be reported in seconds by citizen(s) who know to publicly shout, 'Unattended Bag!' The area would be quickly & calmly cleared by the citizens themselves. But, unfortunately, America hasn't been yet 'hurt enough' by terrorism for their government to fully understand the need to educate its citizens or for the government to understand that it's their citizens who are, inevitably, the best first-line of defense against terrorism.

Aviv also was concerned about the high number of children here in America who were in preschool and kindergarten after 9/11, who were 'lost' without parents being able to pick them up, and about our schools that had no plan in place to best care for the students until parents could get there. (In New York City, this was days, in some cases!)

He stresses the importance of having a plan, that's agreed upon within your family, to respond to in the event of a terrorist emergency. He urges parents to contact their children's schools and demand that the schools, too, develop plans of actions, as they do in Israel. Does your family know what to do if you can't contact one another by phone? Where would you gather in an emergency? He says we should all have a plan that is easy enough for even our youngest children to remember and follow.

Aviv says that the U. S. government has in force a plan that, in the event of another terrorist attack, will immediately cut-off everyone's ability to use cell phones, blackberries, etc., as this is the preferred communication source used by terrorists and is often the way that their bombs are detonated.

How will you communicate with your loved ones in the event you cannot speak? You need to have a plan.

If you believe what you have just read, then you must feel compelled to send to every concerned parent or guardian, grandparents, uncles, aunts, whatever and whomever. Nothing will happen if you choose not to do so, but in the event it does happen, this particular email will haunt you..."I should have sent this to..... ", but I didn't believe it and just deleted it as so much trash from old Bill Jones!!!

REPLY FROM MY UNITED SATES SENATOR SAXBY CHAMBLISS

Thank you for contacting me regarding H.R. 1, the "American Recovery and Reinvestment Act of 2009,"it is good to hear from you.

On January 28, 2009, the House of Representatives voted along party lines to pass this bill and send it to the Senate. As lawmakers worked to amend the legislation, the majority repeatedly discouraged efforts to find solutions that would truly stimulate the economy. Instead of focusing on creating jobs, boosting the housing sector and lending a hand to Americans who have lost jobs through no fault of their own, this massive bill morphed into a bloated government giveaway. It is one of the most expensive pieces of spending legislation ever created. It also expands an already enormous deficit. Therefore, I voted against cutting off debate on the legislation, and against its passage in the Senate. However, the bill passed by a vote of 61-37. On February 13, 2009, I also voted against the conference report of the bill, which ultimately passed by a vote of 60-38.

The majority in Congress has been in runaway mode when it comes to spending taxpayer dollars. This legislation is yet another sign that Washington is more concerned with pet projects than with taxpayers' concerns.

If we do not get a handle on federal spending - including both discretionary and entitlement programs - and make reforms now, we will pass this burden to our children and grandchildren. We must reform our budget process, put an end to wasteful spending and implement the fiscal responsibility that taxpayers demand and deserve.

This registration document, made available on Jan. 24, 2007, By the Fransiskus Assisi school in Jakarta , Indonesia , Shows the registration of Barack Obama under the name Barry Soetoro made by his step-father, Lolo Soetoro.

Name: Barry Soetoro

Religion: <u>Islam</u>

Nationality: <u>Indonesian</u>

How did little Indonesian, Barry Soetoro, (A.K.A. Barack Obama) get around the issue of nationality to become president?

PART 2:

In a move certain to fuel the debate over Obama's qualifications for the presidency, the group "Americans for Freedom of Information" has released copies of Obama's college transcripts from Occidental College. The transcript indicates that Obama, under the name Barry Soetoro, received financial aid as a foreign student from Indonesia as an undergraduate at the school.

The transcript was released by Occidental College in compliance with a court order.

The transcript shows that Obama (Soetoro) applied for financial aid and was awarded a Fellowship for foreign students from the Fulbright Foundation Scholarship program.

To qualify, for the scholarship, a student must claim foreign citizenship.

The news has created a firestorm at the White House as the release casts increasing doubt about Obama's legitimacy and qualification to serve as president.

In a related matter, under growing pressure from several groups, Justice Antonin Scalia announced that the Supreme Court agreed to hear arguments concerning Obama's legal eligibility to serve as President in a case brought by Leo Donofrio of New Jersey.

This lawsuit claims Obama's dual citizenship disqualified him from serving as president.

Donofrio's case is just one of 18 suits brought by citizens demanding proof of Obama's citizenship or qualifications to serve as president. Gary Kreep of the United States Justice Foundation has released the results of their investigation of Obama's campaign spending.

This study estimates that Obama has spent upwards of $950,000 in campaign funds in the past year with eleven law firms in 12 states for legal resources to block disclosure of any of his personal records.

Mr. Kreep indicated that the investigation is still on-going but that the final report will be provided to the U.S. Attorney general, Eric Holder.

Mr. Holder has refused to comment on the matter.

Let other folks know this news the media won't let other folks know this news the media won't embrace! Neither one of the Obama pair had time to get a real job and work for a paycheck We paid the balance on their education and travel.

JUDGMENT DAY...TRIAL REF OBAMA

Federal Judge David Carter sets Trial Date for Obama's Eligibility. The expedited trial has been set for Jan. 26, 2010!

Many concerned veterans and citizens attended the hearing in Federal Court in Santa Ana in the lawsuit against Barack Obama to determine his eligibility to be President and Commander in Chief. About 150 people showed up, almost all in support of the lawsuit to demand that Obama release his birth certificate and other records that he has hidden from the American people.

Judge David Carter refused to hear Obama's request for dismissal. He indicated there was almost no chance that this case would be dismissed. Obama is arguing this lawsuit was filed in the wrong court if you can believe that. Obama would prefer a "kangaroo court" instead of a Federal court! Assuming Judge Carter denies Obama's motion for dismissal, he will likely then order expedited discovery which will force Obama to release his birth certificate in a timely manner (if he has one).

The judge, who is a former U.S. Marine, repeated several times that this is a very serious case which must be resolved quickly so that the troops know that their commander in Chief is eligible to hold that position and issue lawful orders to our military in this time of war. He basically said Obama must prove his eligibility to the court! He said Americans deserve to know the truth about their President!

The two U.S. Attorneys representing Barack Obama tried everything they could to sway the judge that this case was frivolous, but Carter would have none of it and cut them off several times. Obama's attorneys left the courtroom after about the 90 minute hearing looking defeated and nervous.

Great day in America for the U.S. Constitution! The truth about Barack Obama's eligibility will be known fairly soon - Judge Carter practically guaranteed it!

Video from the press conference after the hearing coming soon. Congratulations to plaintiff's attorney! She did a great job and won some huge victories. She was fearless!

This needs to be forwarded to everyone you know...

AXIS OF IDIOTS DID HE MISS ANY?

This retired USMC Sgt. Major has his Stuff together.

Jimmy Carter, you are the father of the Islamic Nazi movement. You threw the Shah under the bus, welcomed the Ayatollah home, and then lacked the spine to confront the terrorists when they took our embassy and our people hostage. You're the "runner-in-chief."

Bill Clinton, you played ring around the Lewinsky while the terrorists were at war with us. You got us into a fight with them in Somalia and then you ran from it. Your weak-willed responses to the USS Cole and the First Trade Center Bombing and Our Embassy Bombings emboldened the killers. Each time you failed to respond adequately, they grew bolder, until 9/11/2001.

John Kerry, dishonesty is your most prominent attribute. You lied about American Soldiers in Vietnam. Your military service, like your life, is more fiction than fact. You've accused our military of terrorizing women and children in Iraq. You called Iraq the wrong war, wrong place, wrong time, and the same words you used to describe Vietnam. You're a fake! You want to run from Iraq and abandon the Iraqis to murderers just as you did to the Vietnamese. Iraq, like Vietnam, is another war that you were for, before you were against it.

John Murtha, you said our military was broken. You said we can't win militarily in Iraq. You accused United States Marines of cold-blooded murder without proof and said we should redeploy to Okinawa. Okinawa, John? And the Democrats call you their military expert! Are you sure you didn't suffer a traumatic brain injury while you were off building your war hero resume? You're a sad, pitiable, corrupt, and washed up old fool. You're not a Marine, sir. You wouldn't amount to a good pimple on a real Marine's butt... You're a phony and a disgrace. Run away, John.

Dick Durbin, you accused our Soldiers at Guantanamo of being Nazis, tenders of Soviet style gulags and as bad as the regime of Pol Pot, who murdered two million of his own people after your party abandoned Southeast Asia to the Communists. Now you want to abandon the Iraqis to the same fate. History was not a good teacher for you, was it? Lord help us! See Dick run.

Nancy Pelosi, Harry Reid, Carl Levine, Barbara Boxer, Diane Feinstein, Russ Feingold, Pat Leahy, Barack Obama, Chuck Schumer, the Hollywood Leftist morons, et al, ad nauseam: Every time you stand in front of television cameras and broadcast to the Islamic Nazis that we went to war because our President lied, that the war is wrong and our Soldiers are torturers, that we should leave Iraq, you give the Islamic butchers - the same ones that tortured and mutilated American Soldiers - cause to think that we'll run away again, and all they have to do is hang on a little longer. It is inevitable that we, the infidels, will have to defeat the Islamic jihadists. Better to do it now on their turf, than later on ours after they have gained both strength and momentum.

American news media, the New York Times particularly: Each time you publish stories about national defense secrets and our intelligence gathering methods, you become one united with the sub-human pieces of camel dung that torture and mutilate the bodies of American Soldiers. You can't strike up the courage to publish cartoons, but you can help Al Qaeda destroy my country. Actually, you are more dangerous to us than Al Qaeda is. Think about that each time you face Mecca to admire your Pulitzer.

You are America's 'AXIS OF IDIOTS.' Your Collective Stupidity will destroy us. Self-serving politics and terrorist-abetting news scoops are more important to you than our national security or the lives of innocent civilians and Soldiers. It bothers you that defending ourselves gets in the way of your elitist sport of politics and your ignorant editorializing. There is as much blood on your hands as is on the hands of murdering terrorists. Don't ever doubt that. Your frolics will only serve to extend this war as they extended Vietnam. If you want our Soldiers home as you claim, knock off the crap and try supporting your country ahead of supporting your silly political aims and aiding our enemies.

Yes, I'm questioning your patriotism. Your loyalty ends with self. I'm also questioning why you're stealing air that decent Americans could be breathing. You don't deserve the protection of our men and women in uniform. You need to run away from this war, this country. Leave the war to the people who have the will to see it through and the country to people who are willing to defend it. Our country has two enemies: Those who want to destroy us from the outside and those who attempt it from within.

Semper Fi,

Sergeant Major, USMC, Retired

This is a savvy man. He has nailed it down pretty good. Too bad it won't do any good. There won't be 1 in 10 that receive it who will forward it.

REPLY FROM MY UNITED SATES SENATOR JOHNNY ISAKSON

Dear Mr. and Mrs. Clark:

Thank you for contacting me regarding H.R.1, the American Recovery and Reinvestment Act of 2009; I appreciate your thoughts and the opportunity to respond.

When President Obama took office he called on Congress to pass a second economic stimulus. The House of Representatives first took up the bill, and it passed by a vote of 244-188. The House-passed stimulus bill is a non-starter for me, as it does not address the core problems that created the current economic crisis and devotes far too much money to programs that will not provide the needed stimulus our economy needs.

Similar concerns arose as the Senate began to amend the House-passed stimulus bill. I worked tirelessly to improve the legislation in a bi-partisan way that was beneficial to the American taxpayer, address the root causes of the problem, and provided tangible stimulus to our economy. In this spirit, I offered an amendment that Sen. Lieberman (I-CT) cosponsored that would provide a tax credit in the amount of $15,000 or 10 percent of the purchase price (whichever is less), with the option to utilize all in one year or spread out over two years. The tax credit would be available to all purchasers of any home from date of enactment for one full year. Buyers must occupy the homes for two years as their principle residences, and taxpayers are able to claim the credit against the 2008 tax return. I was pleased that the Isakson-Lieberman amendment won unanimous support on the Senate floor. I am certain that this tax credit provides positive stimulus for qualified homebuyers to purchase homes and will also invigorate credit markets once again.

During Senate debate numerous Republican alternatives were offered - alternatives that put money directly in the pockets of the American people. I supported these amendments as I feel the American people know how to spend their money more effectively than the government does and will provide the best stimulus to the economy. As the cost and burden on current taxpayers and future generations continued to sky rocket and support for the legislation began to wane, several members worked together to craft a compromise. The compromise, led by Senators Collins (R-ME) and Nelson (D-NE), removed $140 billion in spending from the near trillion dollar bill. Even with the Collins-Nelson agreement, and the reduction in spending, this economic stimulus package devotes too much money to programs that will not provide the stimulus our economy so desperately needs, and too little money to infrastructure and incentives for investment. At a cost of nearly $100,000 in debt for every American family and as the bill primarily spends money on programs that are not stimulative, I could not support the Democratic stimulus bill H.R. 1. Despite my efforts to create a more bipartisan and effective piece of legislation, the stimulus passed the Senate by a vote of 60 to 38 on February 13, 2009.

Unfortunately, during Conference negotiations between the House and Senate on the final stimulus bill, the Isakson-Lieberman homebuyer tax credit that previously won unanimous Senate approval was removed. Instead, the Democrats leading negotiations allowed little Republican input and modified the previously passed first-time homebuyer tax credit from the Housing and Economic Recovery Act of 2008, H.R.3221. In its place, the Democrats inserted a dramatically watered down incentive, which passed the Senate on February 13, 2009, and did the following: it extended the availability of their credit for homes purchased before December 1, 2009; it retained the credit recapture if the house is sold within three years of purchase; it eliminated the repayment obligation for taxpayers that purchased homes after January 1, 2009, it increased the maximum value of the credit to $8,000, and it removed the prohibition on financing by mortgage revenue bonds. In addition, the credit phases out for taxpayers with adjusted gross income in excess of $75,000 ($150,000 in the case of a joint return). Finally, the credit contained in the stimulus bill unfortunately was only for first-time homebuyers purchasing a single-family type home.

As our nation continues to struggle through the current economic crisis it is important to stay focused on the recovery aspects. I believe the key to returning stability to the economy lies within the housing market. We must find a way to keep people in their homes, stabilize foreclosures and return consumer confidence to the marketplace. Once stability comes back to the housing market, you will see investors and small business begin to reinvesting in job creating activities, which will put hard working Americans back to work. I am committed to taking the necessary steps to work with my Senate colleagues to make this come to pass. Our nation has always demonstrated a strong resiliency and I am confident we will once again bounce back stronger than ever, where hard working Americans are at the front lines of economic prosperity.

GUN CONTROL

Barack Obama at a recent rural elementary school assembly in East Texas, asked the audience for total quiet. Then, in the silence, he started to slowly clap his hands once every few seconds, holding the audience in total silence. Then he said into the microphone, "Children, every time I clap my hands together, a child in America dies from gun violence..." Then, little Richard Earl, with a proud East Texas drawl, pierced the quiet and said: "Well, dumb-ass, then stop clapping!"

AND THE MARXISTS APPROVAL RATING STAYS AROUND 60%

Nothing Obamanation does has made much sense, if at all.

It must be very hard for our enemies to fully understand American Liberals. Try to put yourself in their shoes for a moment:

The Obama Administrations National Intelligence Director Dennis Blair, speaking about those prisoners at Guantanamo Bay (GITMO) who are likely to be released in the United States under new policies adopted by Obama, pointed out that the prisoners would have to get some sort of welfare to help them start their new lives in the good old US of A.

Director Blair apparently thought about this quite a lot and concluded, "We can't put them out on the street."

First, you are captured on the battlefield where you are trying to kill U.S. soldiers.

Then you are imprisoned at GITMO and immediately provided expert medical attention and better nutrition than ever before.

Soon lawyers from some of Washington's most prestigious law firms offer to represent you free of charge.

Finally, you are told that the president intends to release you inside the country you dream will be destroyed some day, and the Director of National Intelligence wants you to be paid a stipend by those dreadful infidel taxpayers so that you can adjust to your new life. And just last week, that same president was floating the idea of taking away some health benefits from the soldiers who captured you!

While we ponder the meaning of all this tonight, let's stop by Arlington National Cemetery for a reality check.

Now you tell me there will never be a 2nd American Revolution!

THREE MEN WHO BROUGHT DOWN WALL STREET

Be sure to read the "where they are now"!

Here is a quick look into 3 former Fannie Mae executives who have brought down Wall Street.

1) Franklin Raines: was a Chairman and Chief Executive Officer at Fannie Mae. Raines was forced to retire from his position with Fannie Mae when auditing discovered severe irregularities in Fannie Mae's accounting activities. At the time of his departure The Wall Street Journal noted, " Raines, who long defended the company's accounting despite mounting evidence that it wasn't proper, issued a statement late Tuesday conceding that "mistakes were made" and saying he would assume responsibility as he had earlier promised. News reports indicate the company was under growing pressure from regulators to shake up its management in the wake of findings that the company's books ran afoul of generally accepted accounting

principles for four years." Fannie Mae had to reduce its surplus by $9 billion. Raines left with a "golden parachute valued at $240 Million in benefits. The Government filed suit against Raines when the depth of the accounting scandal became clear. http://housingdoom.com/2006/12/18/fannie-charges/ . The Government noted, "The 101 charges reveal how the individuals improperly manipulated earnings to maximize their bonuses, while knowingly neglecting accounting systems and internal controls, misapplying over twenty accounting principles and misleading the regulator and the public. The Notice explains how they submitted six years of misleading and inaccurate accounting statements and inaccurate capital reports that enabled them to grow Fannie Mae in an unsafe and unsound manner." These charges were made in 2006. The Court ordered Raines to return $50 Million Dollars he received in bonuses based on the miss-stated Fannie Mae profits.

2) Tim Howard: Was the Chief Financial Officer of Fannie Mae. Howard "was a strong internal proponent of using accounting strategies that would ensure a "stable pattern of earnings" at Fannie. In everyday English - he was cooking the books. The Government Investigation determined that, "Chief Financial Officer, Tim Howard, failed to provide adequate oversight to key control and reporting functions within Fannie Mae," On June 16, 2006, Rep. Richard Baker, R-La., asked the Justice Department to investigate his allegations that two former Fannie Mae executives lied to Congress in October 2004 when they denied manipulating the mortgage-finance giant's income statement to

achieve management pay bonuses. Investigations by federal regulators and the company's board of directors since concluded that management did manipulate 1998 earnings to trigger bonuses. Raines and Howard resigned under pressure in late 2004.

Howard's Golden Parachute was estimated at $20 Million!

3) Jim Johnson: A former executive at Lehman Brothers and who was later forced from his position as Fannie Mae CEO. A look at the Office of Federal Housing Enterprise Oversight's May 2006 report on mismanagement and corruption inside Fannie Mae, and you'll see some interesting things about Johnson. Investigators found that Fannie Mae had hidden a substantial amount of Johnson's 1998 compensation from the public, reporting that it was between $6 million and $7 million when it fact it was $21 million."   Johnson is currently under investigation for taking illegal loans from Countrywide while serving as CEO of Fannie Mae. Johnson's Golden Parachute was estimated at $28 Million.

Where are they now?

1) Franklin Raines? Raines works for the Obama Campaign as Chief Economic Advisor

2) Tim Howard?   Howard is also a Chief Economic Advisor to Obama

3) Jim Johnson?   Johnson hired as a Senior Obama Finance Advisor and was selected to run Obama's Vice Presidential Search Committee

If Obama plans on cleaning up the mess - his advisors have the expertise - they made the mess in the first place. Would you trust the men who tore Wall Street down to build the New Wall Street?

THE "WE DESERVE IT DIVIDEND"

I'm against the $85,000,000,000.00 bailout of AIG. Instead, I'm in favor of giving $85,000,000,000 to America in a We Deserve It Dividend!

I'm no math genius, so to make the math simple, let's assume there are 200,000,000 bonafide U.S. Citizens that are 18+ years of age. Our population is about 301,000,000 +/- counting every man, woman and child. So 200,000,000 might be a fair estimate of adults 18 and up.

So divide 200,000,000 adults that are 18+ into $85 billon. That equals $425,000.00. Here's where we all get excited.

My plan is to give $425,000 to every person that is 18+ years of age as a "We Deserve It Dividend". Of course, it would not be tax free. So let's assume a tax rate of 30%. So...Every US Citizen that is 18+ years of age would have to pay $127,500.00 in taxes. That sends $25,500,000,000.00 right back to Uncle Sam. It also means that every adult 18+ years of age has $297,500.00 in their pocket.

A husband and wife have $595,000.00 free and clear!

What would you do with $297,500.00 to $595,000.00 in your family?

Again, back to basics here;

Pay off your mortgage - housing crisis solved. Repay college loans - what a great boost to new grads - put away money for college - it'll be there. Save in a bank - create money to loan to entrepreneurs.

Buy a new car - create jobs. Invest in the market - capital drives growth. Pay for your parent's medical insurance - health care improves. Enable Deadbeat Dads to come clean - or else.

Remember this is for every adult U S Citizen 18+ years of age including the folks who lost their jobs at Lehman Brothers and every other company that is cutting back. Most importantly, really paying those serving in our Armed Forces! If we're going to re-distribute wealth let's really do it...instead of trickling out a puny $1,000.00 ("vote buy") economic incentive that is being proposed by one of our candidates for President.

If we're going to do an $85 billion dollar bailout, let's bail out every adult U S Citizen 18+!

As for the problem companies; AIG - liquidate it. Sell off its parts. Let American General go back to being American General. Sell off the real estate and let the private sector bargain hunters cut it up and clean it up.

Here's my rationale, we deserve it and AIG doesn't.

Sure it's a crazy idea that of course can "never work", but can you imagine the Coast-To-Coast Block Party! How do you spell Economic Boom? I trust my fellow adult Americans to know how to use the $85 Billion "We Deserve It Dividend" more than I do the geniuses at AIG or in Washington DC. And remember, The Family plan only really costs $59.5 Billion because $25.5 Billion is returned instantly in taxes to Uncle Sam!

AND IT WAS IN BALANCE

God was missing for six days. Eventually, Michael, the archangel, found him, resting on the seventh day.

He inquired, 'Where have you been?'

God smiled deeply and proudly pointed downwards through the clouds, 'Look, Michael. Look what I've made.'

Archangel Michael looked puzzled, and said, 'What is it?'

'It's a planet,' replied God, 'and I've put Life on it. I'm going to call it Earth and it's going to be a place to test Balance.'

'Balance?' inquired Michael, 'I'm still confused.'

God explained, pointing to different parts of earth. 'For example, northern Europe will be a place of great opportunity and wealth, while southern Europe is going to be poor. Over here I've placed a continent of white people, and over there is a continent of black people. Balance in all things.'

God continued pointing to different countries. 'This one will be extremely hot, while this one will be very cold and covered in ice.'

The Archangel, impressed by God's work, then pointed to a land area and said, 'What's that one?'

'That's Washington State, the most glorious place on earth. There are beautiful mountains, rivers and streams, lakes, forests, hills, and plains. The people from Washington State are going to be handsome, modest, intelligent, and humorous, and they are going to travel the world. They will be extremely sociable, hardworking, high achieving, and they will be known throughout the world as diplomats, carriers of peace, and producers of software.'

Michael gasped in wonder and admiration, but then asked, 'But what about balance, God? You said there would be balance.'

God smiled as he said, 'There is another Washington. Wait till you see the idiots I put there.'

FELLOW AMERICANS

Please know: I am black; I grew up in the segregated South. I did not vote for Barack Obama; I wrote in Ron Paul's name as my choice for president. Most importantly, I am not race conscious. I do not require a black president to know that I am a person of worth, and that life is worth living. I do not require a black president to love the ideal of America.

I cannot join you in your celebration. I feel no elation. There is no smile on my face. I am not jumping with joy. There are no tears of triumph in my eyes. For such emotions and behavior to come from me, I would have to deny all that I know about the requirements of human flourishing and survival - all that I know about the history of the United States of America, all that I know about American race relations, and all that I know about Barack Obama as a politician. I would have to deny the nature of the "change" that Obama asserts has come to America. Most importantly, I would have to abnegate my certain understanding that you have chosen to sprint down the road to serfdom that we have been on for over a century. I would have to pretend that individual liberty has no value for the success of a human life. I would have to evade your rejection of the slender reed of capitalism on which your success and mine depend. I would have to think it somehow rational that 94 percent of the 12 million blacks in this country voted for a man because he looks like them (that blacks are permitted to play the race card), and that they were joined by self-declared "progressive" whites who voted for him because he doesn't look like them. I would have to be wiping my mind clean of all that I know about the kind of people who have advised and taught Barack Obama and will fill posts in his administration - political intellectuals like my former colleagues at the Harvard University's Kennedy School of Government.

I would have to believe that "fairness" is the equivalent of justice. I would have to believe that a man who asks me to "go forward in a new spirit of service, in a new service of sacrifice" is speaking in my interest. I would have to accept the premise of a man that economic prosperity comes from the "bottom up," and who arrogantly believes that he can will it into existence by the use of government force. I would have to admire a man who thinks the standard of living of the masses can be improved by destroying the most productive and the generators of wealth.

Finally, Americans, I would have to erase from my consciousness the scene of 125,000 screaming, crying, cheering people in Grant Park, Chicago irrationally chanting "Yes We Can!" Finally, I would have to wipe all memory of all the times I have heard politicians, pundits, journalists, editorialists, bloggers and intellectuals declare that capitalism is dead - and no one, including especially Alan Greenspan, objected to their assumption that the particular version of the anti-capitalistic mentality that they want to replace with their own version of anti-capitalism is anything remotely equivalent to capitalism.

So you have made history, Americans. You and your children have elected a black man to the office of the president of the United States, the wounded giant of the world. The battle between John

Wayne and Jane Fonda is over - and that Fonda won. Eugene McCarthy and George McGovern must be very happy men. Jimmie Carter, too. And the Kennedys have at last gotten their Kennedy look-a-like. The self-righteous welfare statists in the suburbs can feel warm moments of satisfaction for having elected a black person. So, toast yourselves: 60s countercultural radicals, 80s yuppies and 90s bourgeois bohemians. Toast yourselves, Black America. Shout your glee Harvard, Princeton, Yale, Duke, Stanford, and Berkeley. You have elected not an individual who is qualified to be president, but a black man who, like the pragmatist Franklin Roosevelt, promises to - Do Something! You now have someone who has picked up the baton of Lyndon Johnson's Great Society. But you have also foolishly traded your freedom and mine - what little there is left - for the chance to feel good. There is nothing in me that can share your happy obliviousness.

95-YEAR OLD WWII BATTLESHIP SAILOR TELLS OBAMA TO "SHAPE UP OR SHIP OUT

This venerable and much honored WW II vet is well known in Hawaii for his seventy-plus years of service to patriotic organizations and causes all over the country. A humble man without a political bone in his body, he has never spoken out before about a government official, until now. He dictated this letter to a friend, signed it and mailed it to the president.

President Obama,

I'm approaching 95 on December 13 of this year. People meeting me for the first time don't believe my age because I remain wrinkle free and pretty much mentally alert.

I enlisted in the U.S. Navy in 1934 and served proudly before, during and after WW II retiring as a Master Chief Bos'n Mate. Now I live in a "rest home" located on the western end of Pearl Harbor, allowing me to keep alive the memories of 23 years of service to my country.

One of the benefits of my age, perhaps the only one, is to speak my mind, blunt and direct even to the head man.

So here goes.

I am amazed, angry and determined not to see my country die before I do, but you seem hell bent not to grant me that wish.

I can't figure out what country you are the president of. You fly around the world telling our friends and enemies despicable lies like: "We're no longer a Christian nation"

"America is arrogant" - (Your wife even announced to the world," America is mean-spirited. " Please tell her to try preaching that nonsense to 23 generations of our war dead buried all over the globe who died for no other reason than to free a whole lot of strangers from tyranny and hopelessness.)

I'd say shame on the both of you, but I don't think you like America, nor do I see an ounce of gratefulness in anything you do, for the obvious gifts this country has given you. To be without shame or gratefulness is a dangerous thing for a man sitting in the White House.

After 9/11 you said, "America hasn't lived up to her ideals." Which ones did you mean? Was it the notion of personal liberty that 11,000 farmers and shopkeepers died for to win independence from the British? Or maybe the ideal that no man should be a slave to another man, those 500,000 men died for in the Civil War? I hope you didn't mean the ideal 470,000 fathers, brothers, husbands, and a lot of fellas I knew personally died for in WWII, because we felt real strongly about not letting any nation push us around, because we stand for freedom.

I don't think you mean the ideal that says equality is better than discrimination. You know the one that a whole lot of white people understood when they helped to get you elected.

Take a little advice from a very old geezer, young man.

Shape up and start acting like an American. If you don't, I'll do what I can to see you get shipped out of that fancy rental on Pennsylvania Avenue. You were elected to lead not to bow, apologize and kiss the hands of murderers and corrupt leaders who still treat their people like slaves.

And just who do you think you are telling the American people not to jump to conclusions and condemn that Muslim major who killed 13 of his fellow soldiers and wounded dozens more. You mean you don't want us to do what you did when that white cop used force to subdue that black college professor in Massachusetts, who was putting up a fight? You don't mind offending the police calling them stupid but you don't want us to offend Muslim fanatics by calling them what they are, terrorists.

One more thing. I realize you never served in the military and never had to defend your country with your life, but you're the Commander-in-Chief now, son. Do your job. When your battle-hardened field General asks you for 40,000 more troops to complete the mission, give them to him. But if you're not in this fight to win, then get out. The life of one American soldier is not worth the best political strategy you're thinking of.

You could be our greatest president because you face the greatest challenge ever presented to any president. You're not going to restore American greatness by bringing back our bloated economy. That's not our greatest threat. Losing the heart and soul of who we are as Americans is our big fight now. And I sure as hell don't want to think my president is the enemy in this final battle.

Sincerely,

A 95-year old hero of the "the Greatest Generation" stands up and speaks out like this. I think we owe it to him to send his words to as many Americans as we can. Please pass it on.

DEMOCRATS

HELLO, DUMMIES!

Oh my God, look at you. Anyone else hurt in the accident? Seriously, Senator Reid has a face of a Saint - A Saint Bernard. Now I know why they call you the arithmetic man. You add partisanship, subtract pleasure, divide attention, and multiply ignorance. Reid is so physically unimposing; he makes Pee Wee Herman look like Mr. T and Reid's so dumb, he makes Speaker Pelosi look like an intellectual. Nevada is soooo screwed! If I were less polite, I'd say Reid makes Kevin Federline look successful.

Speaking of the Speaker...Nancy Pelosi, hubba, hubba! Hey baby, you must've been something before electricity. Seriously, the Speaker may look like an idiot and talk like an idiot but don't let that fool you. She really is an idiot. Madame Speaker...Want to make twelve bucks the hard way? Pelosi says she's not partisan, but her constituents call her Madame Pelossilini.

Charlie Rangel...Still alive and still robbing the taxpayer's blind. What does that make, six decades of theft? Rangel's the only man with a rent-controlled mansion. He's the guy who writes our tax laws but forgot to pay taxes on $75 grand in rental income! So why isn't he the Treasury Secretary? Rangel runs more scams than a Nigerian Banker.

Barney Frank - he's a better actor than Fred Flintstone. Consider...he and Dodd caused the whole financial meltdown and they're not only not serving time with Bubba and Rodney, they're still heading up the financial system! Let's all admit it...Barney Frank slobbers more than a sheepdog on Novocain. How did this guy get elected? Oh, that's right....he's from Massachusetts. That's the state that elects Mr. Charisma, John Kerry -- man of the people!

You know, if Senator Dodd were any more crooked, you could open wine bottles with him. Here's a news flash, Dodd: when your local newspaper calls you a "lying weasel", it may be time to retire. Dodd's involved in more shady deals than the Clintons...Even Rangel looks up to him!

Press Secretary Robert Gibbs, I really respect you...Especially given your upbringing. All you've overcome...I heard your birth certificate is an apology from the condom factory. I don't know what makes you so dumb, but it really works for you. Personally, I don't think you are a fool, but what's my opinion compared to that of thousands of others? Gibbs does his best expositional work in the bathroom every morning.

As for President Obama, what can I say? They say President Obama's arrogant and aloof, but I don't agree. Now it's true when you enter the room, you have to kiss his ring. I don't mind, but he has it in his back pocket. His mind is open to new ideas -- so open that ideas simply pass through it. Obama lies so much, I was actually surprised to find out his first name really was Barack. Just don't ask about his middle name! But Obama was able to set a record...He actually lied more in 60 days than Bill Clinton. As far as his administration -- what with the tax cheat and lobbyists well, in the words of Patches O'Houlihan, "It's like watching a bunch of retards trying to hump a doorknob out there."

With all due respect; for those that voted for "hope and change"...bend over and prepare to receive your bounty.

WAR? WHAT WAR?

War on Terror: The phrase is actually now a misnomer. Iraq and Afghanistan have been rebranded the "Overseas Contingency Operation," and lawyers are being deployed to fight the real battles. The strategy of the new administration looks a lot like the course the Clinton administration set us on before Sept. 11, 2001. And we know how that turned out: Clinton relied on prosecutors to fight terrorists, mistakenly treating terrorism as random crime rather than the grave national security threat that it is.

After each al-Qaida attack that occurred on his watch, Clinton dispatched FBI agents and lawyers overseas to collect evidence. This simply bought Osama bin Laden and his henchmen more time to launch their "Big Bang," as counterterrorism officials call 9/11. Astonishingly, this administration seems to have adopted that failed strategy, which could leave us exposed to an even bigger bang. According to the Los Angeles Times, the Justice Department will now have "a central role in overseas counterterrorism cases."

The administration has expanded its authority to question foreign suspects and gather evidence "to try to ensure that criminal prosecutions are an option." In other words, the FBI is in, the CIA is out, and the Pentagon is gradually being stripped of its war. The Global War on Terror is now a global crime scene. The real battles going forward will be waged inside courtrooms.

The FBI played a lead role in international terrorism investigations before 9/11. Its intelligence proved lousy. The Pentagon and CIA, meantime, have taken the fight to the enemy in their backyard, keeping them off balance. Yet they're being edged out, and the White House has even directed the Pentagon to stop calling what it's doing in Iraq, Afghanistan and other terror fronts a "war."

In a recent e-mail to Pentagon staffers, the Defense Department's office of security review noted "this administration prefers to avoid using the term 'Long War' or 'Global War on Terror.' (GWOT.) Please use 'Overseas Contingency Operation.'" Contingency is code for reacting to trouble, and not going on the offensive — though the aggressive strategy has kept the country free from a major attack for eight years.

In another throwback to the Clinton era, the White House has redirected law enforcement to focus investigations on white supremacist groups.

According to a recent internal report by the Department of Homeland Security, the administration thinks Timothy McVeigh types pose a greater domestic threat than radical Muslims, even though several homegrown terrorism cases have popped up in the last month alone — including Monday's shooting of U.S. soldiers in Little Rock by one Abdulhakim Mujahid Muhammad. DHS was set up after 9/11 to protect the country from Islamic terrorism.

All this comes on top of the administration's plan to close Gitmo and transfer al-Qaida terrorists into the U.S. court system, treating them as if they were criminal defendants and not the enemy combatants they are.

With each passing month, the administration seems to backslide deeper into a dangerous pre-9/11 mentality that puts the nation at increasing risk of attack.

RARE REPORT

A long read but if you take the time you might find it interesting... So aren't we proud of POTUS? Not bloody likely. Goofball! patriots: Much more detail on the Alabama-Obama-Pirate-SEAL Incident. You won't be able to put this down once starting it! Further explains what went on with the Obama -FBI connection to the event.

Real story of Obama (POTUS) and the hostage rescue...

I hope Mxxxx is up and feeling better now-- it's that time of the year for all the spring pollens. And, thanks, my xxxx brief went well Friday.

Your "Real" story is not exactly the way I heard it, and probably has a few political twists thrown in to stir the pot. Rather than me trying to correct it, I'll just tell you what I found out from my contacts at NSWC Norfolk and at SOCOM Tampa.

First though, let me orient you to familiarize you with the "terrain." In Africa from Djibouti at the southern end of the Red Sea eastward through the Gulf of Aden to round Cape Guardafui at the easternmost tip of Africa (also known as "The Horn of Africa") is about a 600 nm transit before you stand out into the Indian Ocean.

That transit is comparable in distance to that from the mouth of the Mississippi at New Orleans to the tip of Florida at Key West— except that 600 nm over there is infested with Somalia pirates. Ships turning southward at the Horn of Africa transit the SLOC (Sea Lane of Commerce) along the east coast of Somalia because of the prevailing southerly currents there. It's about 1,500 nm on to Mombassa, which is just south of the equator in Kenya.

Comparably, that's about the transit distance from Portland Maine down the east coast of the US to Miami Florida. In other words, the ocean area being patrolled by our naval forces off the coast of Somalia is comparable to that in the Gulf of Mexico from the Mississippi River east to Miami then up the eastern seaboard to Maine.

Second, let me globally orient you from our Naval Operating Base in Norfolk, VA, east across the Atlantic to North Africa, thence across the Med to Suez in Egypt, thence southward down the Red Sea to Djibouti at the Gulf of Aden, thence eastward to round Cape Guardafui at the easternmost tip of Africa, and thence southerly some 300 miles down the east cost of Somali out into the high seas of the Indian Ocean to the position of MV Alabama is a little more than 7,000 nm, and plus-nine time-zones ahead of EST.

Hold that thought, in that, a C-17 transport averaging a little better than 400 kts (SOG) takes the best part of 18 hours to make that trip.

In the evening darkness late Thursday night, a team of Navy SEALs from NSWC (Naval Surface Warfare Center) Norfolk parachuted from such a C-17 into the black waters (no refraction of light) of the Indian Ocean-- close-aboard to our 40,000 ton amphibious assault ship, USS Boxer (LHD 4), the flagship of our ESG (Expeditionary Strike Group) in the AOR (Area Of Responsibility, the Gulf of Aden). They not only parachuted in with all of their "equipment," they had their own inflatable boats, RHIB's (Rigid Hull, Inflatable Boats) with them for over-water transport. They went into Boxer's landing dock, debarked, and staged for the rescue-- Thursday night. And, let me comment on time-late: In that the SEAL's quick response-- departing ready-alert in less than 4 hours from Norfolk-- supposedly surprised POTUS's staff, whereas President Obama was miffed not to get his "cops" there before the Navy. He reportedly questioned his staff, "Will 'my' FBI people get there before the Navy does?" It took the FBI almost 12 hours to put together a team and get them packed-up-- for an "at sea" rescue. The FBI was trying to tell him that they are not practiced to do this-- Navy SEALs are.

But, BHO wanted the FBI there "to help," that is, carry out the Attorney General's (his) orders to negotiate the release of Captain Phillips peacefully-- because apparently he doesn't trust GW's military to carry out his "political guidance."

The flight of the FBI's passenger jet took a little less than 14 hours at

500-some knots to get to Djibouti. Boxer's helos picked them up and transported them out to the ship. The Navy SEALs were already there, staged, and ready to act by the time POTUS's FBI arrived on board later that evening. Notably, the first request by the OSC (On Scene Commander) that early Friday morning to take them out and save Captain Phillips was denied? "No, wait until 'my' FBI people get there."

Third, please consider a candid assessment of ability that finds that the FBI snipers had never practiced shooting from a rolling, pitching, yawing, surging, swaying, heaving platform-- and, target-- such as a ship and a lifeboat on the high seas. Navies have been doing this since Admiral Nelson trained "Marines" to shoot muskets from the ship's rigging. Ironically, he was killed at sea in HMS Victory at the Battle of Trafalgar by a French Marine rifleman that shot him from the rigging of the French ship that they were grappling alongside.

Notably, when I was first training at USNA in 1955, the Navy was doing it with a SATU, Small Arms Training Unit, based at our Little Creek amphibian base. Now, Navy SEAL's, in particular SEAL Team six (The "DevGru") based at NSWC (Naval Surface Warfare Center) at Little Creek do that training now, and hone their skills professionally-- daily. Shooting small arms from a ship is more of an accomplished "Art Form" than it is a practiced skill. When you are "in the bubble" and "in tune" with the harmonic motion you find, through practice, that you are "able to put three .308 slugs inside the head of a quarter at 100 meters, in day or night-- or, behind a camouflaged net or a thin enclosure, such as a superstructure bulkhead. Yes, we have the monocular scopes that can "see" heat-- and, draw a bead on it. SEALs are absolutely expert at it-- with the movie clips to prove it.

Okay, now try to imagine patrolling among the boats fishing everyday out on the Grand Banks off our New England coast, and then responding to a distress call from down around the waters between Florida and the Bahamas. Three points for you to consider here: (1) Time-Distance-Speed relationships for ships on the high seas, for instance, at a 25-knot SOA (Speed Of Advance) it takes 24 hours to make good 600 nm-- Bainbridge did. (2) Fishermen work on the high seas and (3) the best place to hide as a "fisherman" pirate is among other fishermen.

Early Wednesday morning, 4/8/2009, MV Alabama is at sea in the IO about 300 miles off the (east) coast of Somalia en route to Mombassa Kenya. Pirates in a small boat start harassing her, and threatening her with weapons. MV Alabama's captain sent out the distress call by radio, and ordered his Engineer to shut down the engines as well as the ship-service electrical generators-- in our lingo, "Go dark and cold." He informed his crew by radio what was happening, and ordered them to go to an out-of-the-way compartment and lock themselves in it-- from the inside. He would stay in the pilot house to "negotiate" with the pirates.

The pirates boarded, captured the Captain, and ordered him to start the engines. He said he would order his Engineer to do so, and he called down to Engine Control on the internal communication system, but got no answer. The lead pirate ordered two of his four men to go down and find him and get the engines started.

Inside a ship without any lights is like the definition of dark. The advantage goes to the people who work and live there. They jumped the two pirates in a dark passageway. Both pirates lost their weapons, but one managed to scramble and get away. The other they tied up, put tape over his mouth and a knife at his throat. Other members of the crew opened the drain cocks on the pirate's boat and cast it adrift. It foundered and sunk. The scrambling pirate made it back to the pilot house and told of his demise. The pirates took the Captain at gun point, and told him to launch one of his rescue boats (not a life boat, per se). As he was lowering the boat for them, the crew appeared with the other pirate to negotiate a trade. The crew let their hostage go too soon, and the pirates kept the captain. But, he purposefully had lowered the boat so it would jam. With the rescue boat jammed, the pirates jumped over to a lifeboat and released it as the captain jumped in the water. They fired at him, made him stop, and grabbed him out of the water. Now, as night falls in the vastness of the Indian Ocean, we have the classic "Mexican" standoff, to wit: A life-boat that is just that, a life-boat adrift without any means of propulsion except oars and paddles; and, a huge (by comparison) Motor Vessel Container Ship adrift with a crew that is not going to leave their captain behind. The pirates are enclosed under its shelter-covering, holding the captain as their hostage. The crew is hunkered down in their ship waiting for the "posse" to arrive.

After receiving MV Alabama's distress call, USS Bainbridge (DDG 96) was dispatched by the ESG commander to respond to Alabama's distress call. At best sustainable speed, she arrived on scene the day after-- that is, in the dark of that early Thursday morning. As Bainbridge quietly and slowly, at darkened-ship without any lights to give her away, arrived on scene, please consider a recorded interview with the Chief Engineer of MV Alabama describing Bainbridge's arrival. He said it was something else "... to see the Navy slide in there like a greyhound!" He then said as she slipped in closer he could see the "Stars and Stripes" flying from her masthead. He got choked up saying it was the "...proudest moment of my life."

Phew! Let that sink in. Earlier in the day, one of the U.S. Navy's Maritime Patrol Aircraft, a fixed wing P3C, flew over to recon the scene. They dropped a buoy with a radio to the pirates so that the Navy's interpreter could talk with the pirates. When Bainbridge arrived, the pirates thought the radio to be a beaconing device, and threw it overboard. They wanted a satellite telephone so that they could call home for help. Remember now, they are fishermen, not "Rocket Scientists," in that; they don't know that we can intercept the phone transmission also.

MV Alabama provided them with a satellite phone. They called home back to "somebody" in Eyl Somalia (so that we now know where you live) to come out and get them. The "somebody" in Eyl said they would be out right away with other hostages, like 54 of them from other countries, and that they would be coming out in two of their pirated ships. Right-- and, the tooth fairy will let you have sex with her. Yea, in paradise. The "somebody" in Eyl just chalked up four more expendables as overhead for "the cost of operation."
 Next page.

Anyway, ESG will continue to "watch" eyl for any ships standing out.

The navy seal team, seal team six, from NSWC briefed the OSC on how they could rescue the captain from the life boat with swimmers-- "combat swimmers," per se. That plan was denied by POTUS because it put the captain in danger-- and, involved killing the pirates.

The FBI negotiators arrived on scene, and talked the pirates into sending their wounded man over for treatment Saturday morning.

Later that afternoon, the SEAL's sent over their RHIB with food and water to recon the life boat but the pirates shot at it. They could have taken them out then (from being fired upon) but were denied again being told that the captain was not in "imminent danger." The FBI negotiators calmed the situation by informing the pirates of threatening weather as they could see storm clouds closing from the horizon, and offered to tow the life boat. The pirates agreed, and Bainbridge took them under tow in their wake at 30 meters-- exactly 30 meters, which is exactly the distance the SEALs practice their shooting skills.

With the lifeboat under tow, riding comfortably bow-down on Bainbridge's wake-wave ("rooster tail") had a 17-second period of harmonic motion, and at the end of every half-period (8.5 seconds) was steady on. The light-enhanced (infra-red heat) monocular scopes on the SEAL's .308 caliber Mark 11 Mod 0 H&K suppressor-fitted sniper rifles easily imaged their target very clearly.

Pirates in a life boat at 30-meters could be compared to fish in a barrel. All that was necessary was to take out the Plexiglas window so that it would not deflect the trajectory of the high velocity .308 round. So, a sniper (one of four) with a wad-cutter round (a flaxen sabot) would take out the window a split second before the kill-shot-- no change in sight-picture, just the window blowing out, clean. Now, here's the part BHO's "whiz kids" knew as well as the Navy hierarchy, including CO Bainbridge and CO Seal Team Six. It's the law in Article 19 of Appendix L in the "Convention of the High Seas" that the Commanding Officer of a US Ship on the high seas is obligated to respond to distress signals from any flagged ship (US or otherwise), and protect the life and property thereof when deemed to be in imminent danger. So, in the final analysis, it would be Captain Castellano's call as to "Imminent Danger," and that he alone was obligated (duty bound) to act accordingly.

Got the picture?

After medically attending to the wounded pirated, and feeding him, come first light (from the east) on Easter Sunday morning and the pirates saw they were being towed further out to sea (instead of westward toward land), the wounded pirate demanded to be returned to the lifeboat. There would be no more negotiations-- and, the four Navy SEAL snipers "in the bubble" went "Unlock." The pirate holding Captain Philips raised the gun to his head, and imminent danger was so observed and noted in the log as CO Bainbridge gave the classic order: weapons released!   I

can hear the echo in my earpiece now, "On my count (from 8.5 seconds), 3, 2, 1," Pop, Bang! Out went the window, followed by three simultaneous shots. The scoreboard flashed: "game over, game over-- Navy 3, Pirates 0!"

I hope you found the above informative as best I know it-- and, please excuse me in that after more than 50 years the Navy is still in me. I submit that America is going to make a comeback, and more than likely it'll be on the back of our cherished youth serving with honor in our military. So, let's Look Up, Get Up -- and, Never Give Up!

God bless our troops, and God save America!

WHO OWNS TARGET?

Ireland View of the Elections

The Irish view things with such beautiful logic and simplicity...

'We in Ireland can't figure out why you people are even bothering to hold a presidential election in the US this year. On one side, you have a bitch who is a lawyer, married to a lawyer, running against a lawyer, who is married to a bitch who is also a lawyer.

On the other side, you have a war hero married to a good looking woman who owns a beer distributorship. What are you lads thinking over there?'

THE DEMOCRATS' EX-PRESIDENTS

Jimmy Carter returned from his visit to Hamas, having embarrassed his country, infuriated the Israelis, and accomplished nothing. The meeting was historic in one sense, marking the first time an American leader actually embraced a head official of a terrorist cult (Nasser Shaer, in Ramallah). Carter told the media that he had solved the problems of the Middle East to his own satisfaction. He was immediately repudiated by Palestinian spokesmen.

Al Gore appears to have taken a break from saving the world, having convinced large numbers of otherwise sensible people that something called "global warming" exists. He can be expected back in short order. Evidence that "warming" has in fact not occurred since 1998 is swiftly becoming public knowledge. Who but St. Al can lead the righteous in beating back this heresy?

Al's former boss, Big Bill, threatens to sink his wife's presidential campaign with every word he utters. But utter them he does, loudly, repeatedly, and without the least visible effort at self-control. You can't make Bill Clinton shut up. He used to be President, you know. Why is it that so many Democratic leaders find it necessary to continue making spectacles of themselves after they leave office?

It's an exclusively Democratic trait -- you don't find Republicans acting this way. The affable Jerry Ford spent his forty years as ex-president in quiet retirement, saving his political commentary for a post-mortem testament. George Bush Sr. may occasionally get the urge to jump out of an airplane, but that's as far as it goes. Even with a son in the Oval Office (and another governing Florida), H.W. has been the soul of self-effacement. Although George W. is constantly savaged in the foulest terms imaginable, H.W. keeps his counsel. WASP stoicism is not yet extinct.

With Ronald Reagan, we have the ideal type of the discreet elder leader. When confronted with his final ordeal by Alzheimer's, he acted the part of the ancient chieftain aware that the tribe must not see its head brought low, and instead retreated to the shadows, to meet his end in dignity and privacy. Examples of such grace and courage do not abound in our epoch.

But with the Dems, it's different. The need for attention and adulation among former Democratic leaders is embarrassing in its nakedness. In almost no other field, in politics or out, can such behavior be found. Only the entertainment world offers a comparable level of pathology.

No more active ex-president exists than Jimmy Carter. He has written a number of books (including a novel and a volume of poetry); he divides his time between Habitat for Humanity, putting up houses across the country, and the Carter Center, monitoring elections across the world. He also engages in personal diplomacy whenever the whim happens to strike him.

This might be harmless if not for Carter's proclivity for thugs. This weakness is often found in educated men, who, apparently out of fear that they've missed out in experiencing some of life's rougher aspects, strike up acquaintances with hard-edged figures they encounter. This goes a long way toward explaining the affection of upper-crust types for the Mumias and Jack Henry Abbots of the world. It also explains the soft spot many hold for self-styled "revolutionaries" such as the Black Panthers, the Weathermen, or the Sandinistas.

As president, Carter had the opportunity to indulge this trait to the fullest. Carter was indirectly responsible for putting the mullahs in power in Iran (kicking off the violent confrontation between Jihadism and the West in the process). He was directly responsible for handing Nicaragua to the Sandinistas (Carter refused to sign off on a plan to replace the dictator Somoza with a government of moderates) and Zimbabwe to Robert Mugabe. (Abel Muzorewa, the centrist opposition figure first elected president, was pushed aside with Carter's acquiescence and a new election arranged that Mugabe was guaranteed to win.)

Carter's weakness for goons has had horrendous historical consequences. Khomeini's takeover of Iran led to a major war in which millions died, the birth of two terror organizations dedicated to the annihilation of Israel, the deaths of thousands of others across the world -- including hundreds of Americans -- and the encouragement of the Jihadi terror movement. The Sandinista takeover resulted in chaos across Central America for over a decade and the slaughter of thousands of Nicaraguans, including a large number of Miskito Indians in a process indistinguishable from genocide. Zimbabwe, once one of the richest states in Africa, is today an economic basket case suffering chronic famine and one of the lowest life expectancies in the world. The end game is being played out now, with a distinct possibility of a climax to rival in horror and blood those of Rwanda and Cambodia.

Carter learned nothing from this, nothing even from his own unprecedented humiliation by the mullahs he helped put into power, who waited until the exact hour of Ronald Reagan's inauguration to release the American hostages they had held for the better part of Carter's last two years in office. To this day, he continues embracing killers, repeating the process endlessly as if, eventually, it'll come out the way he pictures it in his heart of hearts, in some impossible lion-and-lamb reconciliation. But it always ends otherwise, in disgrace for himself and misery for third parties. Yet he cannot see it.

Al Gore's motives are far more prosaic. Embittered by the results of the 2000 election, a hair-thin defeat at the hands of a man he considered his manifest inferior (recall all the sighing and head-shaking during the debates); he cast about at loose ends for awhile, grew a beard, and put on some weight. He had already published one best-seller, Earth in the Balance, a popularization of already widely-known environmentalist truisms. Returning to that well, he latched onto global warming and rode it to glory -- or at least close to it, gathering himself a Nobel and an Oscar (which put him one up on Carter).

Gore has none of Carter's taste for criminals, and his campaign has done considerably less harm to date than Carter's. But in the long run it may well be even more dangerous. Like all Greens, Gore is an authoritarian, his prescriptions having the aura of the people's block committee and the reeducation camp. So it's just as well that the warming thesis has run into cold facts recently. If we are in truth moving into a "quiet sun" period -- a period of dramatically reduced solar activity (as indications suggest we are), then every last puff of CO2 on earth will do nothing to stop the mercury from dropping like a stone. It'll be interesting to see how Gore deals with this. (At least they can't make him give his Nobel back.) But don't count him out -- he's more than a politician; he's an impresario.

Bill Clinton is probably the simplest case of the three, and at the same time the most annoying. Bill simply likes attention -- it doesn't matter where it comes from or how it's expressed. A twenty-year-old intern, crooked businessmen, the Emperor of Antarctica -- it's pretty much the same. Those of us who believe that Liberalism infantilizes its adherents will find a useful exhibit in Bill Clinton.

But at the same time it's harmless. Bill Clinton is never going to court professional killers (except maybe for campaign donations) and is not going off on any crusades. This is due in large part to his other chief characteristic, sloth. If there is any other president more characterized by pathological laziness, the record doesn't reveal it. His entire presidency was a portrait of the effects of least effort carried out to all extremes in every possible case. Least effort in Rwanda, least effort against Osama bin Laden, least effort against Kim Jong-Il. It's even evident in his pickups. Clinton did not go out chasing women; he waited for them to come to him. That's how he ended up with such a harem of oddballs.

Thus is third-millennial Liberalism represented by its major leaders. It didn't used to be this way. Even Harry Truman, nobody's idea of the soul of discretion, knew what was expected of an elder statesman and played his role as required. Nor can one imagine JFK or FDR schmoozing with terrorists or making dubious documentaries. This is something new, a product of the transformed, postmodern Democratic Party.

For forty years, Liberalism has been the ideology of failure. Its last successful program was the civil rights movement, and that was very much a grass roots effort, politicians only jumping aboard as its success became apparent. Since then, in any field you care to name -- foreign policy, the economy, national security -- Liberalism's record has been one of collapse. Even its minor successes, such as NAFTA and welfare reform under Bill Clinton, were initiatives adapted from the GOP.

Consider what kind of psychic impact this must have on individuals with the egos necessary not only to engage in politics, but to rise to the top levels of their party. To serve an ideology that not only cannot succeed, but refuses to allow success, that has become the embodiment of failure of its historical moment. They don't even have the satisfaction of taking a good shot -- contemporary Liberalism does not allow good shots. No sooner are the plans made, the proposals offered, than they wind up in the hands of the ideologues, who want to know how many GLB&T individuals will be involved, who is responsible for the environmental impact statement, and whether it violates the UN Resolution on Cetacean and Chimpanzee Rights. Under such circumstances, courage will not be found, results are a rumor, and success is always going to be just beyond reach.

It must be a bitter pill. And so the Liberal poll demands another turn at the plate, another opportunity to prove himself, to demonstrate to the world that he was right all along. And since he's not alone on stage, since he's competing with somebody else who actually is president at the moment (and may in fact be accomplishing things), he picks the most outlandish, fantastic, comic-book tasks imaginable. Tasks beyond the reach of any single human individual, perhaps any nation. Carter wants to be the universal peacemaker and guarantor of democracy. Gore would like to save the planet. And Bill... in attempting to convince the nation that Hillary is presidential material, he has the most thankless task of all.

Grown men, trying to convince the world that they're supermen - it's sad, and pointless, and more than a little ridiculous.

We'll be seeing more of it. Having accomplished little or nothing, Liberal presidents are going to be left unsatisfied and restless, and will hit the streets in an effort to do something about it. In extreme cases, like that of Jimmy Carter, they are going to blame everyone else in the world but themselves, and make the world pay for it. Now, where did Obama go off to?

57 STATES?

What's in the heart comes out via the tongue!

Hey, folks, you want to tweak the Drive-By Media with me right now?

You are aware, probably, that Barack Obama lost his bearings recently and said that he was going to campaign in all 57 states. You heard this? And everybody chalked it up to, 'Well, he's tired.' You know, this is a Dan Quayle moment. I mean, Dan Quayle goes out there and misspells 'potato,' and we still hear jokes about it. Barack Obama says he's gonna go out and campaign in 57 states, he was just tired, you know, it's been such a long campaign, he's been so many places, he probably thinks there are 57 states.

Well, I have here a printout from a web site called the International Humanist and Ethical Union. And here is how the second paragraph of an article on that website begins.

'Every year from 1999 to 2005 the organization of the Islamic conference representing the 57 Islamic states presented a resolution to the United Nations Commission on human rights called combating.'

Obama said he's going to campaign in 57 states, and it turns out that there are 57 Islamic states. There are 57 Islamic states.

So did Obama just lose his bearings, or was this a more telling slip, ladies and gentlemen?

KEEP IT GOING, FOLKS!

BIG OIL

This is truly the basis of our "oil/gas problem". Along with the fact that our wonderful Congress has prevented the construction of any new refinery since 1976 because of radical environmentalists and other "goofy greenies", we couldn't convert the oil to gas even if we had plentiful oil at a reasonable price.

As usual, to divert the blame away from themselves, Congress claims that the high price of oil is primarily due to Commodities/Futures speculators bidding the price of future oil contracts higher and higher. Hogwash! That's only typical investors/gamblers taking advantage of the stupidity of our Congress and their policies.

Probably the smartest thing we all could do as individuals is to vote each and every incumbent out of the US Congress next November and bring in some intelligent business people---not political jackasses!!

Now, maybe you would like to know what I really think of our Congress!

HERE ARE MY POINTS AND THOUGHTS FOR ALL LIBERALS:

National security - Victory in Iraq; Fully support NSA, Patriot act, tough interrogations, keeping Gitmo open; not demean our military while they are fighting for their Country; i.e. Harry Reid: "the surge has failed", "the war is lost"; Ensure that our veterans can live out their lives in dignity.

Oppose Appeasement - Oppose any and all efforts to negotiate with dictators of the world in places like Iran, Syria, North Korea, Cuba, and Venezuela without "pre-conditions"

Support Tax cuts, and fiscal responsibility - the American people are not under taxed, government spends too much; eliminate and vote against all earmarks; balance the budget

Energy Independence - Drill in Anwar and the 48 states; Building new refineries; Begin building and using Nuclear Facilities; Expand coal mining; Realistic steward of the environment while simultaneously working with private industry to develop the new energy technologies for the future, with the goal being that America becomes completely energy independent within the next 15 years.

Secure our borders completely within 12 months - Build all necessary fences; Use all available technology to help and support agents at the border; Train and hire agents as needed.

Healthcare: - Look for Free-Market solutions to the problems facing the Healthcare industry, and will vigorously oppose any efforts to "nationalize healthcare"; Individual health savings accounts, that includes "catastrophic insurance" for every American, so people can control their own healthcare choices.

Education - "Save" American children from the failing educational system; Fight to break the unholy alliance of the Democratic party and teachers unions, which at best has institutionalized mediocrity, and has failed children across the country; Fight for "CHOICE" in education and let parents decide; fight for vouchers for parents.

Social Security and Medicare - "Save" social security and Medicare from bankruptcy; Options include "private retirement" funds so people can "control" their own destiny.

Judges - Support ONLY judges who recognize that their job is to interpret the Constitution, and NOT legislate from the bench.

American Dream - Duty and responsibility to educate, inform, and remind people that with the blessings of Freedom comes a Great responsibility. That Government's primary goal is to preserve, protect and defend our God given gift of freedom.

That Government's do not have the ability to solve all of our problems, and to take away all of our fears and concerns. We need their pledge that we will promote Individual liberty, Capitalism, a strong national defense and will support policies that encourage such...

It should be our fundamental belief that limited Government, and Greater individual responsibility will insure the continued prosperity and success for future generations.

We the people who believe in the words of Ronald Reagan, that we are "the best last hope for man on this earth," "a shining city on a hill," and that our best days are before us if our Government will simply trust the American people.

A WINNING PLATFORM

Wouldn't it be great to turn on the tv and hear any U.S. president, regardless of political party, give the following speech?

'My Fellow Americans: As you all know, the defeat of
the Iraq regime has been completed.

Since Congress does not want to spend any more money on this war,
our mission in Iraq is complete.

This morning I gave the order for a complete removal of all
American forces from Iraq. This action will be complete within 30
days. It is now time to begin the reckoning.

Before me, I have two lists. One list contains the names of countries
which have stood by our side during the Iraq conflict. This list is
short. The United Kingdom, Spain, Bulgaria, Australia,
and Poland are some of the countries listed there.

The other list contains every one not on the first list. Most of the
world's nations are on that list. My press secretary will be
distributing copies of both lists later this evening.

Let me start by saying that effective immediately, foreign aid to
those nations on List 2 ceases immediately and indefinitely. The
money saved during the first year alone will pretty much pay for the
costs of the Iraqi war...Then every year there after it'll go to our
social security system so it won't go broke in 20 years.

The American people are no longer going to pour money into third
world Hell holes and watch those government leaders grow fat on
corruption.

Need help with a famine?

Wrestling with an epidemic?

Call France.

In the future, together with Congress, I will work to redirect this
money toward solving the vexing social problems we still have at

home. On that note, a word to terrorist organizations. Screw with us and we will hunt you down and eliminate you and all your friends from the face of the earth.

Thirsting for a gutsy country to terrorize?

Try France or maybe China.

I am ordering the immediate severing of diplomatic relations with France, Germany, and Russia. Thanks for all your help, comrades. We are retiring from NATO as well. Bonne chance, mezamies.

I have instructed the Mayor of New York City to begin towing the many UN diplomatic vehicles located in Manhattan with more than two unpaid parking tickets to sites where those vehicles will be stripped, shredded and crushed. I don't care about whatever treaty pertains to this. You creeps have tens of thousands of unpaid tickets. Pay those tickets tomorrow or watch your precious Benzes, Beamers and limos be turned over to some of the finest chop shops in the world. I love New York.

A special note to our neighbors. Canada is on List 2. Since we are likely to be seeing a lot more of each other, you folks might want to try not pissing us off for a change.

Mexico is also on List 2 its president and his entire corrupt government really needs an attitude adjustment. I will have a couple extra thousand tanks and infantry divisions sitting around. Guess where I am going to put 'em? Yep, border security.

Oh, by the way, the United States is abrogating the NAFTA treaty – starting now.

We are tired of the one-way highway. Immediately, we'll be drilling for oil in Alaska-which will take care of this country's oil needs for decades to come. If you're an environmentalist who opposes this decision, I refer you to List 2 above: pick a country and move there. It is time for America to focus on its own welfare and its own citizens. Some will accuse us of isolationism. I answer them by saying, 'darn tootin.'

Nearly a century of trying to help folks live a decent life around the world has only earned us the undying enmity of just about everyone on the planet. It is time to eliminate hunger in America. It is time to eliminate homelessness in America. To the nations on List 1, a final thought. Thank you guys. We owe you and we won't forget.

To the nations on List 2, a final thought:

You might want to learn to speak Arabic.

God bless America...

Thank you and good night.'

LET ME SEE IF I HAVE THIS STRAIGHT?

1) His father was a Kenya, Muslim, black – we have his father was Muslim, black = we have seen pictures of his African family.

2) His mother is a Kansan, atheist; white-where are the pictures of his Kansan, white mother and his white grandparents who raised him?

3) His father deserted his mother and him when he was very young and went back to his family in Kenya

4) His mother married an Indonesian Moslem and took him to Jakarta where he was schooled in a Moslem school

5) His mother returned to Hawaii and he was raised by his white

Kansan. He later went to the best high dollar schools, how?

6) He lives in a $1.4 million dollar white house that he acquired through a deal with a wealthy fundraiser. How?

7) He "worked" as a civil rights activist in Chicago – has never held a productive job. The Presidency is not a civil rights post. Nor is it subject to affirmative action set asides.

8) He entered politics at the state level and then the national level where he has minimal experience

9) He is proud of his "African heritage" but is seems that his only African connection was that his African father got a while girl pregnant and deserted her. I didn't know that sperm carried a "cultural" gene. Where is the price in his white culture?

10) He goes to a "Afro centric" church that hates whites, hates Jews, and blames America for all the world's perceived faults

And then repeatedly covers up for the pastor and the church

He claims that he could not confront his pastor but he wants us to believe that he can confront North Korea and Iran, right!??

Yeah, I think I see how he could be a uniter and bring us together, I think the hope is that he hopes no one will put the pieces together!

Sometimes you get, and sometimes you get got…

POLITICALLY CORRECT?

The following is the 2007 winning entry from an annual contest calling for the most appropriate definition of a contemporary term. This year a definition required for the contemporary term, 'Political Correctness'.

The winner wrote:

"Political Correctness is a doctrine, fostered by a delusional, illogical minority, and rabidly promoted by an unscrupulous mainstream media, which holds forth the proposition that it is entirely possible to pick up a turd by the clean end."

OBAMA EXPLAINS NATIONAL ANTHEM STANCE

Hot on the heels of his explanation for why he no longer wears a flag pin, presidential candidate Senator Barack Obama was forced to explain why he doesn't follow protocol when the National Anthem is played.

According to the United States Code, Title 36, Chapter 10, Sec. 171, "During rendition of the national anthem when the flag is displayed, all present except those in uniform are expected to stand at attention facing the flag with the right hand over the heart.

"As I've said about the flag pin, I don't want to be perceived as taking sides," Obama said. "There are a lot of people in the world to whom the American flag is a symbol of oppression. And the anthem itself conveys a war-like message. You know, the bombs bursting in air and all. It should be swapped for something less parochial and less bellicose. I like the song 'I'd Like to Teach the World to sing.' If that were our anthem, then I might salute it."

Whaaaaaaat!!!!!!!!!! Yes, ladies and gentlemen, this could possibly be our next president. Literally, unbelievable and appalling that any one of this stature could possibly win the Democratic nomination, much less the Presidency of the United States of America!!!!!!

TAKE DOWN THE BIRD FEEDER

I bought a bird feeder. I hung it on my back porch and filled it with seed. What a beauty of a bird feeder it is, as I filled it lovingly with seed. Within a week we had hundreds of birds taking advantage of the continuous flow of free and easily accessible food.

But then the birds started building nests in the boards of the patio, above the table, and next to the barbecue. Then came the poop. It was everywhere: on the patio tile, the chairs, and the tables, everywhere!

Then some of the birds turned mean. They would dive bomb me and try to peck me even though I had fed them out of my own pocket. And others birds were boisterous and loud. They sat on the feeder and squawked and screamed at all hours of the day and night and demanded that I fill it when it got low on food.

After a while, I couldn't even sit on my own back porch anymore. So I took down the bird feeder and in three days the birds were gone. I cleaned up their mess and took down the many nests they had built all over the patio.

Soon, the back yard was like it used to be…quiet, serene and no one demanding their rights to a free meal.

Now let's see…

Our government gives out free food, subsidized housing, free medical care, and free education and allows anyone born here to be an automatic citizen.

Then the illegal's came by the tens of thousands. Suddenly our taxes went up to pay for free services; small apartments are housing 5 families; you have to wait 6 hours to be seen by an emergency room doctor; your child's 2nd grade class is behind other schools because over half the class doesn't speak English.

Corn Flakes now come in a bilingual box; I have to 'press one' to hear my bank talk to me in English, and people waving flags other than 'Old Glory' are squawking and screaming in the streets, demanding more rights and free liberties.

Just my opinion, but maybe it's time for the government to take down the bird feeder.

If you agree, pass it on; if not, continue cleaning up the poop!

THE SNEEZE

They walked in tandem, each of the ninety-two students filing into the already crowded auditorium. With their rich maroon gowns flowing and the traditional caps, they looked almost as grown up as they felt.

The dads swallowed hard behind broad smiles and moms freely brushed away tears.

This class would NOT pray during the commencements; not by choice, but because of a recent court ruling prohibiting it.

The principal and several students were careful to stay within the guidelines allowed by the ruling. They gave inspirational and challenging speeches, but no one mentioned divine guidance and no one asked for blessings on the graduates or their families.

The speeches were nice, but they were routine until the final speech received a standing ovation.

A solitary student walked proudly to the microphone. He stood still and silent for just a moment, and then it happened.

All 92 students, every single one of them, suddenly sneezed!

The student on stage simply looked at the audience and said, 'God bless you'.

And he walked off stage. The audience exploded into applause. This graduating class had found a unique way to invoke God's blessing on their future with or without the court's approval.

Isn't this a wonderful story? Pass it on to all your friends and God bless you!

This is a true story. It happened at the University of Maryland.

RESPONSE TO THE SNEEZE:

This ruling (not recent by the way) was made by a Liberal (Democrat) judge appointed by Liberal (Democrat) elected 'officials'; this is exactly the same as the 5-liberial judges on the United States Supreme Court (all of whom were appointed by elected 'Democrat officials') who ruled last week that the terrorists caught on the battle

field and currently held in US military jails should have the same constitutional rights as the people they are trying to kill – that would be everyone reading this email. The same fools that have voted these elected Democratic officials to office will indeed make sure Obama gets elected – since he has promised "have hope…change is coming" – change indeed. Wow.

So as cute and heartwarming as this story appears, it should never have been required – all 'Democrat officials' elected to office labor to have God removed from all walks of our life – and then, when we need God the most, those same elected 'officials' and the Liberal media push their way to the front screaming we all need to pray for God's blessing.

Hypocritical? Indeed.

By the way…the four Supreme Court judges who voted the terrorists should NOT have our constitutional rights were appointed by Republican presidents who support God in all walks of our life.

WHAT A BLACK COLUMNIST HAS TO SAY ABOUT OBAMA

It's an amazing time to be alive in America. We're in a year of firsts in this presidential election: the first viable woman candidate; the first viable African-American candidate; and, a candidate who is the first front running freedom fighter over 70. The next president of America will be a first.

We won't truly be in an election of firsts, however, until we judge every candidate by where they stand. We won't arrive where we should be until we no longer talk about skin color or gender. Now that Barack Obama steps to the front of the Democratic field, we need to stop talking about his race, and start talking about his policies and his politics.

The reality is this: Though the Democrats will not have a nominee until August, unless Hillary Clinton drops out, Mr. Obama is now the frontrunner, and its time America takes a closer and deeper look at him. Some pundits are calling him the next John F. Kennedy. He's not. He's the next George McGovern. And it's time people learned the facts.

Because the truth is that Mr. Obama is the single most Liberal senator in the entire U.S. Senate. He is more Liberal than Ted

Kennedy, Bernie Sanders, or Mrs. Clinton. Never in my life have I seen a presidential frontrunner whose rhetoric is so far removed from his record. Walter Mondale promised to raise our taxes, and he lost. George McGovern promised military weakness, and he lost. Michael Dukakis promised a Liberal domestic agenda, and he lost.

Yet Mr. Obama is promising all those things, and he's not behind in the polls. Why? Because the press has dealt with him as if he were in a beauty pageant. Mr. Obama talks about getting past party, getting past red and blue, to lead the United States of America. But let's look at the more defined strokes of who he is underneath this superficial "beauty."

Start with national security, since the president's most important duties are as commander-in-chief. Over the summer, Mr. Obama talked about invading Pakistan, a nation armed with nuclear weapons; meeting without preconditions with Mahmoud Ahmadinejad, who vows to destroy Israel and create another Holocaust; and Kim Jong II, who is murdering and starving his people, but emphasized that the nuclear option was off the table against terrorists - something no president has ever taken off the table since we created nuclear weapons in the 1940s. Even Democrats who have worked in national security condemned all of those remarks. Mr. Obama is a foreign-policy novice who would put our national security at risk.

Next, consider economic policy. For all its faults, our health care system is the strongest in the world. And free trade agreements, created by Bill Clinton as well as President Bush, have made more goods more affordable so that even people of modest means can live a life that no one imagined a generation ago. Yet Mr. Obama promises to raise taxes on "the rich." How to fix Social Security? Raise taxes. How to fix Medicare? Raise taxes. Prescription drugs? Raise taxes. Free college? Raise taxes. Socialize medicine? Raise taxes. His solution to everything is to have government take it over. Big Brother on steroids, funded by your paycheck.

Finally, look at the social issues. Mr. Obama had the audacity to open a stadium rally by saying, "All praise and glory to God!" but says that Christian leaders speaking for life and marriage have "hijacked" - hijacked - Christianity. He is pro-partial birth abortion, and promises to appoint Supreme Court justices who will rule any restriction on it unconstitutional. He espouses the abortion views of Margaret Sanger, one of the early advocates of racial cleansing. His spiritual leaders endorse homosexual marriage, and he is moving in that direction. In Illinois, he refused to vote against a statewide ban on all handguns in the state. These are radical left, Hollywood, and San Francis co values, not Middle America values.

The real Mr. Obama is an easy target for the general election. Mrs. Clinton is a far tougher opponent. But Mr. Obama could win if people don't start looking behind his veneer and flowery speeches. His vision of "bringing America together" means saying that those who disagree with his agenda for America are hijackers or warmongers. Uniting the country means adopting his Liberal agenda and abandoning any conflicting beliefs.

But right now everyone is talking about how eloquent of a speaker he is and - yes - they're talking about his race. Those should never be the factors on which we base our choice for president. Mr. Obama's radical agenda sets him far outside the American mainstream, to the left of Mrs. Clinton.

It's time to talk about the real Barack Obama. In an election of firsts, let's first make sure we elect the person who is qualified to be our president in a nuclear age during a global civilizational war.

CHAUFFEUR

Nancy was being driven through the countryside by her chauffeur when suddenly, a cow jumps out into the road, they hit it full on, and the car comes to a stop.

Nancy, in her usual charming manner, says to the chauffeur: 'You get out and check - you were driving.' The chauffeur gets out, checks, and reports that the animal is dead but it was old. You were driving; go and tell the farmer,' says Nancy.

Two hours later, the chauffeur returns totally plastered, hair ruffled with a big grin on his face.

'My God, what happened to you?' asks Nancy.

The chauffeur replies: 'When I got there, the farmer opened his best bottle of malt whisky, the wife gave me a slap-up meal and the daughter made love to me.'

'What on earth did you say?' asks Nancy. 'I just knocked on the door and when it was answered, I said to them: 'I'm Nancy Pelosi's chauffeur, and I've just killed the old cow.'

MLK WAS A REPUBLICAN

On this day of reflection and celebration, let us not forget what MLK preached: judge a man not by the color of his skin, but rather by the content of his character.

MLK was, indeed, both a Black Man and a Republican; both of these are facts. He was as much Republican as he was Black. Neither of these facts can be disputed.

Also, it is requested that you forward it to as many left wing socialists as you know or as you can. Hopefully, you know some blacks whom require additional education. Blacks today will celebrate a man whose wisdom they do not follow; they judge their leader today by the color of his skin; because they are the true definition of idiot by continuing to judge their leader by the content of his character.

Enjoy... Happy MLK Day!

SENIOR DEATH WARRANTS

Send this around again as a reminder to all Americans.

In England anyone over 59 cannot receive heart repairs or stents or bypass because it is not covered as being too expensive and not needed.

Obama wants to have a health care system just like Canada's and England's.

I got this today and am sending it on. If Obama's plans in other areas don't scare you, this should. Please do not let Obama sign senior death warrants. Everybody that is on this mailing list is either a senior citizen, is getting close or knows somebody that is.

Most of you know by now that the Senate version (at least) of the "stimulus" Bill includes provisions for extensive rationing of health care for senior citizens.

The author of this part of the bill, former senator and tax evader, Tom Daschle, was credited by Bloomberg with the following statement: Bloomberg: Daschle says "health-care reform will not be pain free. Seniors should be more accepting of the conditions that come with age instead of treating them."

If this does not sufficiently raise your ire, just remember that our esteemed Senators and Congressmen have their own healthcare plan that is first dollar or very low co-pay which they are guaranteed the remainder of their lives and are not subject to this new law if it passes.

Please use the power of the Internet to get this message out. Talk it up at the grassroots level. We have an election coming up in one year and nine months. And we have the ability to address and reverse the dangerous direction the Obama administration and its allies have begun and in the interim, we can make their lives miserable.

Let's do this!   If you disagree, do nothing.

So True

"BAIL'EM OUT!!!????

Hell, back in 1990, the Government seized the Mustang Ranch brothel in Nevada for tax evasion and, as required by law, tried to run it... They failed and it closed. Now, we are trusting the economy of our country, our banking system, our auto industry and possibly our health plans to the same nit-wits who couldn't make money running a whore house and selling whiskey?!"

"What are we thinking?

Barack Hussein Obama: I told you so, yes I did…

Montreal, Quebec, Canada

When Obama won the presidency with the help of the leftist media, Hollywood and entertainment Liberals, ethnic socialists (ACORN), stupid non-business professionals and Bush haters, I wrote: It won't take six months until the people figure this guy out and realize how horrible a mistake they've made. And when they come to that realization, the damage to the United States of America will be so great it will take a generation or more to repair - if ever.

The idiots who not only voted for the messiah, but also worked hard to promote his lordship, are now left holding the bag.

Here are two things they will never do: they will never admit to making a blunder out of all proportion by electing a snake-oil salesman with no positive social history or management experience of any kind. They will never take responsibility for the curse they've imposed upon the immediate and long-term future of their country.

In essence, the people responsible for putting this horror show in power are themselves responsible for every cataclysmic decision he makes and the consequences thereof.

In just six months, the messiah's polls are showing the following: on Healthcare Reform, he's going under for the third time with polling well under 50 percent, even within his own party. Even though he might be able to muscle a Healthcare Reform Bill by using Chicago bully tactics against his fellow Democrats, it will just make things worse.

On Cap and Trade (Cap and Tax), the fat lady is already singing. On the Stimulus Package (Tax and Spend), his popularity is in free fall. On the TARP package he took and ran with from President Bush, it's all but Good-Night Irene. On the closing of GITMO and "his" war on what he no longer wants called the War on Terrorism, he's standing in quicksand with his head just about to go under. On a comparison between himself and George W. Bush at the same six months into their respective first term presidencies, Bush is ahead of him in the polls. On a comparison between "he who walks on water" and the 12 preceding Presidents between WW II and now, Obama ranks 10th. On a poll just conducted, that asks who you would vote for today between Obama and Mitt Romney, it's a dead heat. Between Obama and Palin, Obama's only ahead by 8 points and she hasn't even begun to campaign!

It seems to me that Obama wants to be everywhere he shouldn't be. He's personally invested in totally insulting America's only real Middle Eastern ally (Israel) in favor of Palestinian despots and murderers. He's traveling the world apologizing for the USA while lecturing others on how to do it right, when in fact and truth he has no experience at doing anything other than getting elected.

He went to the Muslim world in Egypt to declare that America "is not a Christian nation" while he heaped praises on Islam, where he compared the "plight" of the Palestinians to the Holocaust.

The Russians think he's a putz. The French think he's rude. The Germans want him to stop spending. The Indians want him to get his nose out of their environmental business. The North Koreans think he's a joke. The Iranians won't acknowledge his calls. And the

British can't even come up with a comprehensive opinion of him. As for the Chinese, he's too frightened to even glance their way. (After all, China now owns a large portion of the United States.)

Maybe if America's first emperor would stay home more, travel less, and work a little bit instead of being on television just about every day (or forget about his Wednesday date nights with his Amazon wife) or stop running to "papered" Town Hall Meetings, perhaps he would have a little bit of time to do the work of the nation.

In all fairness, it wasn't hard to be right in my prediction concerning Obama's presidency, even in its first six months, so I'm going to make yet another prediction: Obama will probably not finish his 4-year term, at least not in a conventional way.

He is such a political horror show, and so detrimental to the USA and his own Democratic party, that the Democrats themselves will either force him to resign or figure out a way to have him thrown out. Who knows, maybe he really isn't a born US citizen and that's a way the Democrats will be able to get rid of him.

or, more likely than not, the Democrats will make Obama their own lame duck president.

I don't believe the Democrats have nearly as much love for their country as they do for their own political fortunes. And with Obama, their fortunes are rapidly becoming toast.

The Democrats can keep on blaming Bush for everything, but that game's already begun to wear real thin.

Their mantra was "we don't want 4 more years," which the stupid people bought, since McCain was nothing at all like George W. Bush. The new mantra will soon become: "we don't anymore."

THIS ONE GOT ME THINKING

It's a slow day in Mamou, Louisiana. The sun is beating down, and the streets are deserted. Times are tough, everybody is in debt, and everybody lives on credit.

On this particular day a traveling salesman from Shreveport is driving through town.

He stops at the Hotel Cazan and lays a $100 bill on the desk saying he wants to inspect the rooms upstairs in order to pick one in which to spend the night.

As soon as the man walks upstairs, Bosco, the owner, grabs the bill and runs next door to pay his debt to Boudreaux the butcher.

Boudreaux takes the $100 and runs down the street to retire his debt to Trosclair, the pig farmer.

Trosclair takes the $100 and heads off to pay his bill at T-Boy's Farmer's Co-op, the local supplier of feed and fuel.

T-Boy at the Farmer's Co-op takes the $100 and runs to pay his debt to the local prostitute, Clarisse, who has also been facing hard times and has had to offer her "services" on credit.

Clarisse rushes to the hotel and pays off her room bill with Bosco, the hotel owner.

Bosco then places the $100 back on the counter so the traveling salesman will not suspect anything.

At that moment the salesman comes down the stairs, picks up the $100 bill, states that the rooms are not satisfactory, pockets the money, and leaves town.

No one produced anything. No one earned anything. However, the whole town is now out of debt and now looks to the future with a lot more optimism.

And that, my friends, is how the United States Government is conducting business today...!!!

1938 AUSTRIA -- LAND OF "THE SOUND OF MUSIC" STORY: MUST, MUST READ!

What I am about to tell you is something you've probably never heard or read in history books.

I am an eyewitness to history. I cannot tell you that Hitler took Austria by tanks and guns; it would distort history. We elected him by a landslide – 98% of the vote. I've never read that in any American publications. Everyone thinks that Hitler just rolled in with his tanks and took Austria by force.

In 1938, Austria was in deep Depression. Nearly one-third of our workforce was unemployed. We had 25% inflation and 25% bank loan interest rates.

Farmers and business people were declaring bankruptcy daily. Young people were going from house to house begging for food. Not that they didn't want to work; there simply weren't any jobs. My mother was a Christian woman and believed in helping people in need. Every day we cooked a big kettle of soup and baked bread to feed those poor, hungry people – about 30 daily.

The Communist Party and the National Socialist Party were fighting each other. Blocks and blocks of cities like Vienna , Linz , and Graz were destroyed. The people became desperate and petitioned the government to let them decide what kind of government they wanted.

We looked to our neighbor on the north, Germany , where Hitler had been in power since 1933. We had been told that they didn't have unemployment or crime, and they had a high standard of living. Nothing was ever said about persecution of any group -- Jewish or otherwise. We were led to believe that everyone was happy. We wanted the same way of life in Austria . We were promised that a vote for Hitler would mean the end of unemployment and help for the family. Hitler also said that businesses would be assisted, and farmers would get their farms back. Ninety-eight percent of the population voted to annex Austria to Germany and have Hitler for our ruler.

We were overjoyed, and for three days we danced in the streets and had candlelight parades. The new government opened up big field kitchens and everyone was fed.

After the election, German officials were appointed, and like a miracle, we suddenly had law and order. Three or four weeks later, everyone was employed. The government made sure that a lot of work was created through the Public Work Service.

Hitler decided we should have equal rights for women. Before this, it was a custom that married Austrian women did not work outside the home. An able-bodied husband would be looked down on if he couldn't support his family. Many women in the teaching profession were elated that they could retain the jobs they previously had been required to give up for marriage.

Hitler Targets Education – Eliminates Religious Instruction for Children:

Our education was nationalized. I attended a very good public school.. The population was predominantly Catholic, so we had religion in our schools. The day we elected Hitler (March 13, 1938), I walked into my schoolroom to find the crucifix replaced by Hitler's picture hanging next to a Nazi flag. Our teacher, a very devout woman, stood up and told the class we wouldn't pray or have religion anymore. Instead, we sang "Deutschland, Deutschland, Uber Alles," and had physical education.

Sunday became National Youth Day with compulsory attendance. Parents were not pleased about the sudden change in curriculum. They were told that if they did not send us, they would receive a stiff letter of warning the first time. The second time they would be fined the equivalent of $300, and the third time they would be subject to jail. The first two hours consisted of political indoctrination. The rest of the day we had sports. As time went along, we loved it. Oh, we had so much fun and got our sports equipment free. We would go home and gleefully tell our parents about the wonderful time we had.

My mother was very unhappy. When the next term started, she took me out of public school and put me in a convent. I told her she couldn't do that and she told me that someday when I grew up, I would be grateful. There was a very good curriculum, but hardly any fun – no sports, and no political indoctrination. I hated it at first but felt I could tolerate it. Every once in a while, on holidays, I went home. I would go back to my old friends and ask what was going on and what they were doing. Their loose lifestyle was very alarming to me. They lived without religion. By that time unwed mothers were glorified for having a baby for Hitler. It seemed strange to me that our society changed so suddenly. As time went along, I realized what a great deed my mother did so that I wasn't exposed to that kind of humanistic philosophy.

Equal Rights Hits Home:

In 1939, the war started and a food bank was established. All food was rationed and could only be purchased using food stamps. At the same time, a full-employment law was passed which meant if you didn't work, you didn't get a ration card, and if you didn't have a card, you starved to death. Women who stayed home to raise their families didn't have any marketable skills and often had to take jobs more suited for men.

Soon after this, the draft was implemented. It was compulsory for young people, male and female, to give one year to the labor corps. During the day, the girls worked on the farms, and at night they returned to their barracks for military training just like the boys. They were trained to be anti-aircraft gunners and participated in the signal corps. After the labor corps, they were not discharged but were used in the front lines. When I go back to Austria to visit my family and friends, most of these women are emotional cripples because they just were not equipped to handle the horrors of combat. Three months before I turned 18, I was severely injured in an air raid attack. I nearly had a leg amputated, so I was spared having to go into the labor corps and into military service.

Hitler Restructured the Family Through Daycare:

When the mothers had to go out into the work force, the government immediately established child care centers. You could take your children ages 4 weeks to school age and leave them there around-the-clock, 7 days a week, under the total care of the government. The state raised a whole generation of children. There were no motherly women to take care of the children, just people highly trained in child psychology. By this time, no one talked about equal rights. We knew we had been had.

Health Care and Small Business Suffer Under Government Controls: Before Hitler, we had very good medical care. Many American doctors trained at the University of Vienna .. After Hitler, health care was socialized, free for everyone. Doctors were salaried by the government. The problem was, since it was free, the people were going to the doctors for everything. When the good doctor arrived at his office at 8 a.m., 40 people were already waiting and, at the same time, the hospitals were full. If you needed elective surgery, you had to wait a year or two for your turn. There was no money for research as it was poured into socialized medicine. Research at the medical schools literally stopped, so the best doctors left Austria and emigrated to other countries.

As for healthcare, our tax rates went up to 80% of our income. Newlyweds immediately received a $1,000 loan from the government to establish a household. We had big programs for families. All day care and education were free. High schools were taken over by the government and college tuition was subsidized. Everyone was entitled to free handouts, such as food stamps, clothing, and housing.

We had another agency designed to monitor business. My brother-in-law owned a restaurant that had square tables. Government officials told him he had to replace them with round tables because people might bump themselves on the corners. Then they said he had to have additional bathroom facilities. It was just a small dairy business with a snack bar. He couldn't meet all the demands. Soon, he went out of business. If the government owned the large businesses and not many small ones existed, it could be in control. We had consumer protection. We were told how to shop and what to buy. Free enterprise was essentially abolished. We had a planning agency specially designed for farmers. The agents would go to the farms, count the live-stock, and then tell the farmers what to produce, and how to produce it.

"Mercy Killing" Redefined:

In 1944, I was a student teacher in a small village in the Alps . The villagers were surrounded by mountain passes which, in the winter, were closed off with snow, causing people to be isolated. So people intermarried and offspring were sometimes retarded. When I arrived, I was told there were 15 mentally retarded adults, but they were all useful and did good manual work. I knew one, named Vincent, very well. He was a janitor of the school. One day I looked out the window and saw Vincent and others getting into a van. I asked my superior where they were going. She said to an institution where the State Health Department would teach them a trade, and to read and write. The families were required to sign papers with a little clause that they could not visit for 6 months. They were told visits would interfere with the program and might cause homesickness.

As time passed, letters started to dribble back saying these people died a natural, merciful death. The villagers were not fooled. We suspected what was happening. Those people left in excellent physical health and all died within 6 months. We called this euthanasia.

The Final Steps - Gun Laws:

Next came gun registration. People were getting injured by guns. Hitler said that the real way to catch criminals (we still had a few) was by matching serial numbers on guns. Most citizens were law abiding and dutifully marched to the police station to register their firearms. Not long after-wards, the police said that it was best for everyone to turn in their guns. The authorities already knew who had them, so it was futile not to comply voluntarily.

No more freedom of speech. Anyone who said something against the government was taken away. We knew many people who were arrested, not only Jews, but also priests and ministers who spoke up. Totalitarianism didn't come quickly, it took 5 years from 1938 until 1943, to realize full dictatorship in Austria .. Had it happened overnight, my countrymen would have fought to the last breath. Instead, we had creeping gradualism. Now, our only weapons were broom handles. The whole idea sounds almost unbelievable that the state, little by little eroded our freedom.

After World War II, Russian troops occupied Austria . Women were raped, preteen to elderly. The press never wrote about this either. When the Soviets left in 1955, they took everything that they could, dismantling whole factories in the process. They sawed down whole orchards of fruit, and what they couldn't destroy, they burned. We called it The Burned Earth. Most of the population barricaded themselves in their houses. Women hid in their cellars for 6 weeks as the troops mobilized. Those who couldn't; paid the price. There is a monument in Vienna today, dedicated to those women who were massacred by the Russians. This is an eye witness account.

"It's true....those of us who sailed past the Statue of Liberty came to a country of unbelievable freedom and opportunity.

America Truly is the Greatest Country in the World. Don't Let Freedom Slip Away.

"After America , There is No Place to Go"

Please forward this message to other voters who may not have it.

TAPS

If any of you have ever been to a military funeral in which taps was played; this brings out a new meaning of it. Here is something Every American should know. We in the United States have all heard the haunting song, 'Taps.' It's the song that gives us the lump in our throats and usually tears in our eyes. But, do you know the story behind the song? If not, I think you will be interested to find out about its humble beginnings.

Reportedly, it all began in 1862 during the Civil War, when Union Army Captain Robert Ellicombe was with his men near Harrison's Landing in Virginia. The Confederate Army was on the other side of the narrow strip of land. During the night, Captain Ellicombe heard the moans of a soldier who lay severely wounded on the field. Not knowing if it was a Union or Confederate soldier, the Captain decided to risk his life and bring the stricken man back for medical attention. Crawling on his stomach through the gunfire, the Captain reached the stricken soldier and began pulling him toward his encampment.

When the Captain finally reached his own lines, he discovered it was actually a Confederate soldier, but the soldier was dead. The Captain lit a lantern and suddenly caught his breath and went numb with shock. In the dim light, he saw the face of the soldier. It was his own son. The boy had been studying music in the South when the war broke out. Without telling his father, the boy enlisted in the Confederate Army. The following morning, heartbroken, the father asked permission of his superiors to give his son a full military burial, despite his enemy status. His request was only partially granted.

The Captain had asked if he could have a group of Army band members play a funeral dirge for his son at the funeral. The request was turned down since the soldier was a Confederate. But, out of respect for the father, they did say they could give him only one musician. The Captain chose a bugler. He asked the bugler to play a series of musical notes he had found on a piece of paper in the pocket of the dead youth's uniform.

This wish was granted. The haunting melody, we now know as 'Taps' used at military funerals was born:

Day is done

Gone the sun

From the lakes

From the hills

From the sky

All is well

Safely rest

God is nigh

Fading light

Dims the sight

And a star

Gems the sky

Gleaming bright

From afar

Drawing nigh

Falls the night

Thanks and praise

For our days

Neath the sun

Neath the stars

Neath the sky

As we go

This we know

God is nigh

I too have felt the chills while listening to 'Taps' but I have never seen all the words to the song until now.

I didn't even know there was more than one verse. I also never knew the story behind the song and I didn't know if you had either so I thought I'd pass it along. I now have an even deeper respect for the song than I did before.

Remember Those Lost and Harmed While Serving Their Country. Also Remember Those Who Have Served and Returned; and for those presently serving in the Armed Forces.

RIGHTEOUSNESS

Last night, in the deep bowels of Hell…, around 10 PM our time, Satan walked over to a fat, seedy looking minion toiling away shoveling more coal into the giant furnaces. He tapped the tormented soul on the shoulder and whispered, "Oh, by the way Teddy, a Republican just won your Senate seat".

GREAT QUOTE

"The danger to America is not Barack Obama but a citizenry capable of entrusting a man like him with the presidency. It will be easier to limit and undo the follies of an Obama presidency than to restore the necessary common sense and good judgment to an electorate willing to have such a man for their president. The problem is much deeper and far more serious than Mr. Obama, who is a mere symptom of what ails us. Blaming the prince of the fools should not blind anyone to the vast confederacy of fools that made him their prince. The republic can survive a Barack Obama. It is less likely to survive a multitude of fools such as those who made him their president." – Author unknown

MORE FACTS

Here are some more facts… not 'feelings' (remember that 1+1 does = 2; regardless of how much you may disagree or how it makes you 'feel'):

Folks...we already got a taste of some change! Let's review…....
George W. Bush (W the president) has been in office for 7 1/2 years. The first six the economy was fine.

A little over one year ago:

1) Consumer confidence stood at a 2 1/2 year high;

2) Regular gasoline sold for $2.19 a gallon;

3) The unemployment rate was 4.5%.

4) the dow jones hit a record high--14,000 +

5) American's were buying new cars, taking cruises, vacations overseas, generally living large!

But American's wanted 'change'!

So, in 2006 they voted in a Democratic Congress & yep--we got 'CHANGE' all right!

1) Consumer confidence has plummeted;

2) Gasoline is now over $4 a gallon & climbing!

3) Unemployment is up to 5% (a 10% increase);

4) Americans have seen their home equity drop by $12 trillion dollars & prices still dropping;

5) 1% of American homes are in foreclosure.

As I write, the dow is probing another low~~11,300--$2.5 trillion dollars has evaporated from their stocks, bonds & mutual funds investment portfolios!

yep, in 2006 America voted for change!...and we sure as hell got it!!!...now 'no-bo', the dem's candidate for president--and the polls say he's gonna be 'the man'--claims he's gonna really give us change!!...just how much more 'change' do ya think you can stand???.... shameful!!

You Liberals are a bunch of cry baby idiots – man up and have the strength to face the truth!! I had dinner last week with an 81-year old who when he was 17 was the tail gunner of a B29 flying missions over Germany in WWII. I thanked him for his service and for my freedom, apologized for the pussy-ass Liberal Americans of today and then bought his dinner. You Liberals can kiss my Conservative ass!! Weeeeeeeeeeeeeeeeeeeee

---

WANT THE TRUTH ABOUT ANWR?

From an ignorant Liberal:

"So, what's your point? Bush and his band of idiots have been in office for 8 years... his dad... Reagan...lots of time for the GOP to drill and help the situation. They've done a great job...don't you think?"

Response from a fact based Conservative:

"Your buddy Cal is rather clueless; the Democrats controlled Congress for 40-years until the Republicans took control of Congress in 1994, who then passed legislation in early 1996 (1-year after taking control), and Clinton vetoed any drilling in this area. A president, Bush, Bush, Reagan do not generate legislation; it was Clinton, 'his' band of idiots, the tree-huggers, the environmental whackos and the new "green" lovers who won't have the drilling. Also keep in mind the drive-by far left media behind these ignorant bastards.

These same moron Liberals will have you believe they have released permits to 68-million acres in the gulf to drill – the truth is, this represents less than 5% of the available land mass to drill, and it is the most undesirable area to drill due to the depth of the water and the costs associated to extract the oil. What babbling bullshit this is. Furthermore, have your buddy Cal help you understand that Cuba and China are scheduled to begin drilling 60-miles off of our gulf coastline and we can't. I do not believe Cuba and China's EPA standards are equal to ours. Why would they give a shit about our coastline? The idiots in paragraph 2 are behind this.

70% of the electricity in France is generated by nuclear power by power plants built by American companies using American technology and development. I can't recall the last nuclear incident in France, oh that's right, there hasn't been one. The 3-mile island incident is 30-years old. We've come a long way baby – we need to build many new nuclear power plants and fire them up. What's that you say? Oh yeah, your buddy Cal and his cronies won't have any of that.

If we processed the existing nuclear waste we currently have, we could provide enough energy for every home in America for the next 32-years. You don't hear that from the drive-by far left media. I could go on and on. It gets old talking and listening to ignorance from people like your buddy Cal; he needs an education."

NO SENSE

A change to what Steve, socialism, when world history has proven socialism won't work? Change to the USA of KKK America? Change to friendship to those that have bombed US government facilities, and state that they wish they had bombed more? Change to "God Damn America"? Change to the mindset that Middle Americans "cling" to their religions and firearms out of ignorance? Change to higher and higher taxes? Change to a national healthcare system that shows it cannot possibly work? Change to the security that provides you and your family the opportunity to live the life you "choose" to live? Perhaps a change BACK to the days in the 90's where our technology secrets were sold to our enemies for fundraising dollars. Or, perhaps a change back to the 90's where our military and defense was cut to the bone. Apparently change to the continuing growth of cradle-to-grave entitlement minded "Democrats" would be a good thing. I believe it would not be a good thing.

I believe in lower taxes, in smaller government, in free enterprise, in a strong military, and the opportunity to be and do anything I choose. I believe I should be able to go the doctor that I choose. I believe the current Congress's approval rating (elected in 11/06 because the "American people have spoken") of a whopping 13% speaks for itself and is well deserving. I believe this Congress (Reid and Pelosi) desire this country to fail. I believe this Congress's San Francisco's left-wing kook mentality is exactly what change will bring to our doorstep. I believe the war we are fighting will continue either where the battle currently is or in my front yard. I believe these "terrorists" don't give a damn where they kill me or my family. I believe a "cut-and-run" philosophy will deliver these terrorists to my family. I believe in capital punishment. I believe in simple right and wrong. I believe a convicted felon of murder should receive the exact same punishment as he/she delivered. I believe in pro-life. I believe in accountability and responsibility. I believe in public hangings. I do not believe in a cradle-to-grave support mechanism such as a federal government. I saw a bumper sticker not long ago which read – "Liberalism: French for Coward", and I agree. I believe John F. Kennedy, Sam Nunn and Zell Miller to be "true Democrats" – compare these three to the current "Democrat" mentality in Congress and tell me you can't see the difference. I believe the difference to be shooting a bullet and throwing a bullet. Listen to John F. Kennedy's 1964 speech, and then listen to his murdering brother Ted speak today. I believe that Jimmy Carter should call it quits and keep his mouth shut - I believe him to be an embarrassment to my country. I believe First Amendment Rights should be taken away from the "main-stream media" and a gag-order be placed on them from reporting any world news. I believe there to be a problem with the 80% of black (I apologize, African-American) children born to fatherless homes. I believe there to be a problem when a white person says anything to or about a black person to which that person does not like or believe, and then the white person becomes a raciest bigot. I believe there to be a problem that the US prison system population consists of over 75% of blacks. I also believe if these people are actually "from" Africa, that they would be outraged and up in arms over the mass-killings of blacks (I apologize, African-Africans) in Africa by other blacks – does this mean it is ok that blacks kill blacks, but I, as a white, cannot say anything to or about a black that they do not want to hear or agree with? I believe the surge has worked. I believe that the "main-stream media" 'chooses' not to report any positive results from our military in a time of war. I believe this same media reported (over-and-over mind you) that the number of American soldier casualties in Iraq in January 2007 as 37 dead – I believe the number of murders in the fine city of Detroit alone in the month of

January 2007 as 35; and that is only ONE American city. Another city, mind you, made up and run by, cradle-to-grave entitlement minded "Democrats".

Liberalism IS a mental disorder:

Saturday, February 16, 2008

WorldNet Daily Exclusive

Top shrink concludes Liberals are nuts!

Makes case ideology is mental disorder

"Based on strikingly irrational beliefs and emotions, modern Liberals relentlessly undermine the most important principles on which our freedoms were founded. "Like spoiled, angry children, they rebel

against the normal responsibilities of adulthood and demand that a parental government meet their needs from cradle to grave."

Say what you want about the current administration, while understanding I am not driving the Bush bandwagon – I would much rather have an administration who will protect my way of life, rather than one that will not.

The two "Democratic" nominees are as dangerous to this country as any one person on the face of this planet. Either one of these two combined with the current Congress will generate results far worse than any scary nightmare you have ever had. I also believe that McCain is not the right answer, just the better wrong answer.

I'm pleased to know that we share one common belief – our Second Amendment Rights. However, rest assured, this also will change. Believe what you choose, and I'll believe what I choose… while we still can. Times…they be a changin… very scary indeed.

Whew…time for a change is right…change back to the basics of what has made this country great. I believe your change has this country on the highway to hell in the hammer lane headed off a cliff. Hope all is well with you and Bobby, have a great day.

AN IDEA WHOSE TIME HAS COME

For too long we have been too complacent about the workings of Congress. Many citizens had no idea that members of Congress could retire with the same pay after only one term, that they didn't pay into Social Security, that they specifically exempted themselves from many of the laws they have passed (such as being exempt from any fear of prosecution for sexual harassment) while ordinary citizens must live under those laws. The latest is to exempt themselves from the Healthcare Reform that is being considered...in all of its forms. Somehow, that doesn't seem logical. We do not have elite that are above the law. I truly don't care if they are Democrat, Republican, Independent or whatever. The self-serving must stop. This is a good way to do that. It is an idea whose time has come.

Have each person contact a minimum of twenty people on their Address list; in turn ask each of those to do likewise.

In three days, most people in The United States of America will have the message. This is one proposal that really should be passed around.

Proposed 28th Amendment to the United States Constitution:

"Congress shall make no law that applies to the citizens of the United States that does not apply equally to the Senators and/or

Representatives; and, Congress shall make no law that applies to the Senators and/or Representatives that does not apply equally to the citizens of the United States".

SPELLING TEST

How's this for a quick education A Short Spelling Lesson:

The last four letters in American…I CAN

The last four letters in Republican…I CAN

The last four letters in Democrats…RATS

End of Lesson!

A MOST INTERESTING EDITORIAL, THE TIDE IS TURNING.

On President Obama:

The Liberal written media is beginning to flip on Obama. From their lips and pens to God's ears!

This writer was a supporter of Barack Obama during his run for the Presidency. This is a staggering appraisal of the President's first year in office- coming from someone who supported President Obama.

AN EDITOR IN CHIEF HAD THIS TO SAY:

Obama's ability to connect with voters is what launched him. But what has surprised me is how he has failed to connect with the voters since he's been in office.

He's had so much overexposure. You have to be selective. He was doing five Sunday shows. How many press conferences? And now people stop listening to him. He's lost his audience. He has not rallied public opinion. He has plunged in the polls more than any other public figure since we've been using polls. He's done everything wrong. Well, not everything, but the major things. I don't consider it a triumph. I consider it a disaster!? And that's what his friends are saying about him.

As the boy president occupied the White House on January 20, 2009 it was predictable that his presidency would last a year, at most, because the things he promised and the things he stood for were so uniquely un-American. Looking back over his year in office, any reasonably precocious fourth grader could make a cogent argument in opposition to nearly everything he's done. In fact, his policies have been so extreme and so far outside the mainstream that he was destined to achieve the most spectacular fall from grace of any American president in history. It was easy to see him serving out the final three years of his term as a virtual exile in the White House, afraid to venture out among any but the most rabid partisans.

Seeing his most ambitious initiative, healthcare reform, die in the flames of the Massachusetts Massacre, Obama made a hastily-planned "sortie" to Ohio for yet another Bush-bashing, self-aggrandizing stump speech on job creation. It was vintage Obama, full of left wing hyperbole and planted questions from the Kool-Ade drinkers in the hand-picked audiences, but there were just two things wrong with it: 1) Almost everything he said was either wrong or an outright lie, and 2) He is so overexposed that no one in the television audience really wanted to see him.

Obama Kool-Aide drinkers in the media, and elsewhere, like to describe Obama as a very bright man, a true intellectual (compared to George W. Bush and Sarah Palin, of course).? If that is the case, why has he demonstrated such a great inability to learn from his failures? The strident words and the in-your-face attitude of his Ohio speech were proof that he has totally misread the meaning of the Scott Brown victory in Massachusetts.

Whatever hopes and dreams he had for his time in the White House, whatever grandiose plans he had for transforming the United States from a constitutional republic with a free market economy into a socialist dictatorship with a centrally planned economy, were all lost on Tuesday, January 19, 2010, one day short of a full year in office. Yet, he appears to have learned nothing from the experience. Comedian George Gobel once asked, rhetorically, "Did you ever get the feeling that the world was a tuxedo and you were a pair of brown shoes?"? In the context of 21st century American politics, and assuming that he has any capacity at all for honest self-examination, Obama must be feeling today very much like a pair of brown shoes at a black tie soiree.

When a politically naive and totally inexperienced young black man, with a glib tongue and an exceptional ability to read words convincingly from a teleprompter, announced that he was ready to serve as President of the United States, Liberals and Democrats saw it as a perfect opportunity to expiate whatever white guilt they may have felt, which was apparently considerable among those on the political left. It didn't seem to bother them that, as one pundit has remarked, every time he walks into a room he is the least experienced and the least qualified man in the room.? Nevertheless, his friends in the worldwide socialist movement and the international banking community figured out how to smuggle hundreds of millions of dollars in illegal campaign funds into the country, the black community rallied to his banner, and American Liberals and the

mainstream media jumped on board the bandwagon. Together, they made it happen for him. But now, just one year later, Obama appears destined to become the unhappiest man in American politics, unhappier than even former Senator John Edwards, who runs a close second, and former president Bill Clinton.

Clinton will be the third unhappiest man because, after capturing the big prize, he frittered away whatever chance he had of ever being compared favorably with Franklin D. Roosevelt as one of the 20th century's greatest Democratic presidents. Not only was he a politician of unusual skill and insight, he was widely known as a policy wonk, among policy wonks, and he had the drive and the personal charm to be loved and respected around the world. Unfortunately, he was never able to put the public trust at the top of his priority list. Instead, he surrounded himself with a large cadre of trusted enablers who allowed him to conduct himself as if he were, not the President of the United States, but the class stud on an extended spring break in Acapulco.

Now that he's been out of office for nearly a decade and he's married to the current Secretary of State, he spends his days trying to find something useful to do without calling an undue amount of attention to himself. Having lied so shamelessly to the American people, having perjured himself in a court of law, having turned the Oval Office into a sexual playpen, and having suffered the humiliation of impeachment, he's smart enough to know that he has little reputation left to protect. So in order to protect whatever legacy remains, he walks a tightrope every day, and he has many more years to walk it without falling off.

Former Senator John Edwards is destined to be the second unhappiest man in American politics because he will be known forever as the most thoroughly despised scumbag in the political arena. A trial lawyer, Edwards amassed a $60 million fortune by winning large jury awards against doctors, hospitals, and corporations. His specialty was cases in which children were born with cerebral palsy, which he blamed on doctors who had waited too long to perform C-sections, a claim that doctors and medical researchers have described as "junk science".? Then, like Obama, he decided that his experience in the courtroom, his glib tongue, and his one term in the U.S. Senate qualified him to be President of the United States. He entered the 2004 Democratic presidential primaries, raising an incredible amount of money for a newcomer to elective office, most of it raised illegally by bundlers, in plaintiff's law firms across the country. He was unsuccessful in his quest for the Democratic nomination but was selected by his Senate colleague, John Kerry, as his running mate.

Two years later, in 2006, Edwards met a young blonde film producer, and embarked on a love affair with her. On February 27, 2008, she gave birth to a daughter, for whom Edwards has consistently denied paternity, until now.

Taking into account that all of this was happening while his wife was waging a long battle with breast cancer, Edwards now has the well-deserved reputation of being the sleaziest of the sleazy. He is so universally despised that, if he is on the lookout for a friend, he might as well resign himself to getting a dog, or moving in with O.J. Simpson. Terry Moran, host of ABC's This Week, put it all in perspective. He said, "What's interesting to note is that Edwards' latest admission (that he is the father of Hunter's child) came while he was in Haiti. As if the people of that sad place didn't have enough problems.? Clearly, the one thing Clinton and Edwards share that places them near the top of our list is their sexual peccadilloes, a shortcoming that Obama does not appear to share with them, at least from what we know so far.

What we do know about Obama is that, since his teen years, he has been mentored by, gravitated toward, and surrounded by the most dangerous sort of America-hating socialists, communists, and Marxists, from Frank Marshall Davis and Saul Alinsky to Weather Underground terrorists Bill Ayers and Bernadine Dohrn, to Rev. Jeremiah Wright, George Soros, and countless radical left college professors

What destines Obama for the top spot on the list of unhappiest American politicians, aside from the failure of his economic recovery program, the failure of his radical cap-and-trade proposal, his failed attempt to give labor bosses unprecedented power to intimidate blue collar workers, and his ill-fated attempt at healthcare reforms, is the fact that he carries on his shoulders the hopes and aspirations of every black child in America. It is unfortunate that, because he is so far outside the American mainstream, and because he carries so much hatred in his heart for the country he seeks to lead, his failures will be viewed by generations of black children, not as the failure of a black socialist attempting to bring down a constitutional republic, but simply as the failure of a black man.

A man can fail in the eyes of his countrymen and still be dearly loved by those closest to him. But in Obama's case, his wife and his two daughters will be there to suffer every agonizing step of his fall along with him. And for the rest of his life, each time he looks into their eyes, and into the eyes of black people everywhere, he will see the crushing disappointment that his ill-fated attempt at national transformation has caused them.

He will be the country's unhappiest man, living the rest of his life knowing that his daughters know that the whole world sees him as a failure. He is simply the wrong man, in the wrong job, in the wrong country, at the wrong time in history.

TOP REASONS I VOTE DEMOCRAT

1) I voted Democrat because I believe oil companies' profits of 4% on a gallon of gas are obscene but the government taxing the same gallon of gas at 15% isn't.

2) I voted Democrat because I believe the government will do a better job of spending the money I earn than I would.

3) I voted Democrat because freedom of speech is fine as long as nobody is offended by it.

4) I voted Democrat because I'm way too irresponsible to own a gun, and I know that my local police are all I need to protect me from murderers and thieves.

5) I voted Democrat because I believe that people who can't tell us if it will rain on Friday can tell us that the polar ice caps will

melt away in ten years if I don't start driving a Prius.

6) I voted Democrat because I'm not concerned about the slaughter of millions of babies through abortion so long as we keep all death row inmates alive.

7) I voted Democrat because I think illegal aliens have a right to free health care, education, and social security benefits.

8) I voted Democrat because I believe that business should not be allowed to make profits for themselves. They need to break even and give the rest away to the government for redistribution as the Democrats see fit.

9) I voted Democrat because I believe Liberal judges need to rewrite the constitution every few days to suit some fringe kooks who would never get their agendas past the voters.

THANK GOD FOR OBAMA THIS IS A MUST READ FOR ALL AMERICANS

Written by an 82-year-old very wise lady; she gives us a whole new slant on the amazing job Obama is doing:

That is right - I will say it "(thank God for the president)."

1) He destroyed the Clinton Political Machine - Driving a stake thru the heart of Hillary's Presidential aspirations - something no Republican was ever able to do. Remember when a Hillary Presidency scared the daylights out of you!

2) He killed off the Kennedy Dynasty - No more Kennedy's trolling Washington looking for booze and women wanting rides home. American women and Freedom are safer tonight!

3) He is destroying the Democratic Party before our eyes!

4) Dennis Moore had never lost a race - quit

5) Evan Bayh had never lost a race - quit

6) Byron Dorgan - had never lost a race – quit

7) These are just a handful of the Democrats whose political careers Obama has destroyed! By the end of 2010 dozens more will be gone!

8) In December of 2008 the Democrats were on the rise. In the last two election cycles they had picked up 14 Senate seats and 52 house seats. The press was touting the death of the Conservative Movement and the Republican Party. In just one year, Obama put a stop to all of this and will probably give the house, if not the Senate back to the Republicans.

9) He has completely exposed Liberals and progressives for what they are. Every Generation seems to need to relearn the lesson on why they should never actually put Liberals in charge. He is bringing home the lesson very well! Liberals tax, borrow and spend. Liberals won't bring themselves to protect America. Liberals want to take over the economy. Liberals think they know what is best for everyone. Liberals aren't happy till they are running your life.

10) He has brought more Americans back to conservatism than anyone since Reagan. In One year he rejuvenated the Conservative movement and brought out to the streets millions of Freedom Loving Americans. Name me one other time in your life that you saw your friends and neighbors this interested in taking back America!

11) His amazing leadership has sparked the greatest period of sales

of firearms and ammunition this country has seen. Law abiding citizens have rallied and have provided a "stimulus" to the sporting goods field while other industries have failed, faded or moved off-shore!

12) In all honesty one year ago I was more afraid than I had ever been in my life. Not of the economy but of the direction our country was going. I thought Americans had forgotten what this country was all about. My neighbors, friends, strangers proved to me that my lack of confidence of the Greatness and Wisdom of the American people was flat out wrong.

13) When the American People wake up no smooth talking teleprompter reader can fool them!

Barak Obama woke up these Great Americans! Again I want to say Thank you Barak Obama! This is exactly the kind of hope and change we desperately needed.

THOSE WITH CLASS

The doctor had his TV on in his office when the news of the military base shootings at Ft. Hood, TX came on. The husband of one of his employees was stationed there.

He called her into his office and as he told her what had happened, she got a text message from her husband saying, "I am okay." Her cell phone rang right after she read the message. It was an ER nurse," I'm the one who just sent you a text, not your husband. I thought it would be comforting but I was mistaken in doing so. I am sorry to tell you this, but your husband has been shot 4 times and he is in surgery."

The soldier's wife left Southern Clinic in Dothan, AL and drove all night to Ft. Hood. When she arrived, she found out her husband was out of surgery and would be OK. She rushed to his room and found that he already had visitors there to comfort him.

He was just waking up and found his wife and the visitors by his side. The nurse took this picture.

What? No news crews and cameras? This is how people with class respond and pay respect to those in uniform.

I sent my cousin in Fayetteville, N.C. (Retired from Special Forces) that picture of Geo. W. visiting the wounded at Ft. Hood.

I got this reply:

"What is even better is the fact George W. Bush heard about Fort Hood, got in his car without any escort, apparently they did not have time to react, and drove to Fort Hood. He was stopped at the gate and the guard could not believe who he had just stopped. Bush only asked for directions to the hospital then drove on. The gate guard called that "The President is on Fort Hood and driving to the hospital."

The base went bananas looking for Obama. When they found it was Bush, they immediately offered escort. Bush simply told them to shut up and let him visit the wounded and the dependents of the dead. He stayed at Fort Hood for over six hours, and was finally asked to leave by a message from the White House.

Obama flew in days later and held a "photo" session in a gym, and did not even go to the hospital.

All this I picked up from two soldiers here who happened to be at Fort Hood when it happened.

This Bush/Obama/Ft. Hood story is something that should be sent to every voter in the US. Those who wanted "change" certainly got it.

PSALM 2009

Obama is the shepherd I did not want

He leadeth me beside the still factories

He restoreth my faith in the Republican party

He guideth me in the path of unemployment for his party's sake

Yea, though I walk through the valley of the bread line

I shall fear no hunger, for his bailouts are with me

He has anointed my income with taxes,

My expenses runneth over

Surely, poverty and hard living will follow me all the days of my life,

And I will live in a mortgaged home forever

I am glad I am American,

I am glad that I am free

But I wish I was a dog...

And Obama was a tree...

Your auto industry, your banks, your health care, your taxes and your freedom of speech

---

GUESS WHO?

Thicker than thieves...this crap never ends...

Edward "Ed" Mezvinsky, born January 17, 1937, is a former

Congressman. A Democrat, he represented Iowa's

1st Congressional district in the United States House of

Representatives for two terms, from 1973 to 1977.

In March 2001, Mezvinsky was indicted and later pleaded guilty to 31 of 69 charges of bank fraud, mail fraud, and wire fraud. Nearly $10 million was involved in the crimes. Shortly after his indictment, he was diagnosed with bipolar disorder, but the judge at his trial disallowed a mental illness defense. After serving five years in federal prison, he was released in April 2008. He is expected to remain on federal probation until 2011, and owes substantial restitution to his victims.

Who exactly is "Ed" Mezvinsky?

He's Chelsea Clinton's new Father-in-Law.

THE ANALOGY

Monkeys

Start with a cage containing five monkeys. Inside the cage, hang a banana on a string and place a set of stairs under it. Before long, a monkey will go to the stairs and start to climb towards the banana. As soon as he touches the stairs, spray all the other monkeys with cold water. After a while another monkey makes the attempt with same result, all the other monkeys are sprayed with cold water. Pretty soon when another monkey tries to climb the stairs, the other monkeys will try to prevent it.

Now, put the cold water away. Remove one monkey from the cage and replace it with a new one. The new monkey sees the banana and wants to climb the stairs.

To his shock, all of the other monkeys beat the snot out of him. After another attempt and attack, he knows that if he tries to climb the stairs he will be assaulted.

Next, remove another of the original five monkeys and replace it with a new one.

The newcomer goes to the stairs and is attacked. The previous newcomer takes part in the punishment with enthusiasm.

Likewise, replace a third original monkey with a new one, then a fourth, then the fifth. Every time the newest monkey takes to the stairs he is attacked.

Most of the monkeys that are beating him up have no idea why they were not permitted to climb the stairs OR even why they are participating in the beating of the newest monkey. Finally, after replacing all of the original monkeys, none of the remaining monkeys have ever been sprayed with cold water. Nevertheless, no monkey ever again approaches the stairs to try for the banana.

Why not?

Because as far as they know, that is the way it has always been done around here.

And that, my fellow monkeys, is how Congress operates - And precisely why we need to replace all the original monkeys this November.

READ THIS...

Very quietly Obama's citizenship case reaches the Supreme Court. In a move certain to fuel the debate over Obama's qualifications for the presidency, the group "Americans for Freedom of Information" has released copies of President Obama's college transcripts from Occidental College. Released today, the transcript school indicates that Obama, under the name Barry Soetoro, received financial aid as a foreign student from Indonesia as an undergraduate. The transcript was released by Occidental College in compliance with a court order in a suit brought by the group in the Superior Court of California. The transcript shows that Obama (Soetoro) applied for financial aid and was awarded a fellowship for foreign students from the Fulbright Foundation Scholarship program. To qualify, for the scholarship, a student must claim foreign citizenship.

This document would seem to provide the smoking gun that many of Obama's detractors have been seeking. Along with the evidence that he was first born in Kenya and there is no record of him ever applying for US citizenship, this is looking pretty grim. The news has created a firestorm at the White House as the release casts increasing doubt about Obama's legitimacy and qualification to serve as President article titled, "Obama Eligibility Questioned," leading some to speculate that the story may overshadow economic issues on Obama's first official visit to the U.K. In a related matter, under growing pressure from several groups, Justice Antonin Scalia announced that the Supreme Court agreed on Tuesday to hear arguments concerning Obama's legal eligibility to serve as President in a case brought by Leo Donofrio of New Jersey. This lawsuit claims Obama's dual citizenship disqualified him from serving as president. Donofrio's case is just one of 18 suits brought by citizens demanding proof of Obama's citizenship or qualification to serve as president.

Gary Kreep of the United States Justice Foundation has released the results of their investigation of Obama's campaign spending. This study estimates that Obama has spent upwards of $950,000 in campaign funds in the past year with eleven law firms in 12 states for legal resources to block disclosure of any of his personal records. Mr. Kreep indicated that the investigation is still ongoing but that the final report will be provided to the U...S. Attorney general, Eric Holder. Mr. Holder has refused to comment on the matter... Let other folks know this news, the media won't!

SUBJECT: RE: ISSUE OF PASSPORT?

While I've little interest in getting in the middle of the Obama birth issue, Paul Hollrah over at FSM did so yesterday and believes the issue can be resolved by Obama answering one simple question: What passport did he use when he was shuttling between New York, Jakarta, and Karachi?

So how did a young man who arrived in New York in early June 1981, without the price of a hotel room in his pocket, suddenly come up with the price of a round-the-world trip just a month later?

And once he was on a plane, shuttling between New York, Jakarta, and Karachi, what passport was he offering when he passed through Customs and Immigration?

The American people not only deserve to have answers to these questions, they must have answers. It makes the debate over Obama's citizenship a rather short and simple one.

Q: Did he travel to Pakistan in 1981, at age 20?

A: Yes, by his own admission.

Q: What passport did he travel under?

A: There are only three possibilities.

1) He traveled with a U.S... Passport,

2) He traveled with a British passport, or

3) He traveled with an Indonesia passport.

Q: Is it possible that Obama traveled with a U.S. Passport in 1981?

A: No. It is not possible. Pakistan was on the U.S... State Department's "no travel" list in 1981.

Conclusion: When Obama went to Pakistan in 1981 he was traveling either with a British passport or an Indonesian passport.

If he were traveling with a British passport that would provide proof that he was born in Kenya on August 4, 1961, not in Hawaii as he claims. And if he were traveling with an Indonesian passport that would tend to prove that he relinquished whatever previous citizenship he held, British or American, prior to being adopted by his Indonesian step-father in 1967.

Whatever the truth of the matter, the American people need to know how he managed to become a "natural born" American citizen between 1981 and 2008.

Given the destructive nature of his plans for America, as illustrated by his speech before Congress and the disastrous spending plan he has presented to Congress, the sooner we learn the truth of all this, the better.

If you care then forward this to as many patriotic Americans as you can, because our country is being looted and ransacked!

THEODORE ROOSEVELT'S IDEAS ON IMMIGRANTS AND BEING AN AMERICAN IN 1907:

'In the first place, we should insist that if the immigrant who comes here in good faith becomes an American and assimilates himself to us, he shall be treated on an exact equality with everyone else, for it is an outrage to discriminate against any such man because of creed, or birthplace, or origin But this is predicated upon the person's becoming in every facet an American, and nothing but an American....There can be no divided allegiance here. Any man who says he is an American, but something else also, isn't an American at all. We have room for but one flag, the American flag... We have room for but one language here, and that is the English language... And we have room for but one sole loyalty and that is a loyalty to the American people.'

Theodore Roosevelt 1907

Every American citizen needs to read this!

A GREAT SPORTS STORY

The stimulus at work!

Some have said that the stimulus hasn't saved any jobs, but here is a case where at least one job was saved.

Take for instance Oregon State University Athletic Director Bob DeCarolis.

Now Mr. DeCarolis was considering firing their Basketball Coach Craig Robinson after an 8 -11 start (2-5) in the Pac 10 conference).

When word reached Washington , Undersecretary of Education Martha Kanter was dispatched to Corvallis with $17 million in stimulus money for the university.

Thankfully, Craig Robinson's job is safe for another year

Now comes the interesting part of our story...

For those of you unfamiliar with Coach Robinson, he just so happens to be the brother in law of none other than our country's beloved President, now you're catching on...

That's right he is the brother of Michelle Obama!

But hey, can't we all come to the conclusion that Coach Robinson's job security was all just a coincidence?

I'm sure of it... Unfucking believable!!

FOX NEWS REPORTING

"If you check President Obama's last trip over-seas, his wife left just after their visit to France. She has yet to accompany him to any Arab country. Think about it. Why is Michelle returning to the states when 'official' trips to foreign countries generally include the First Lady."

Here's one thought on the matter:

While in a Blockbuster renting videos I came across a video called "Obama". There were two men standing next to me and we talked about President Obama. These guys were Arabs, so I asked them why they thought Michele Obama headed home following the President's recent visit to France instead of traveling On to Saudi Arabia and Turkey with her husband. They told me she could not go to Saudi Arabia , Turkey or Iraq . I said "Why not? Laura Bush went to Saudi Arabia , Turkey and Dubai ." They said that Obama is a Muslim and therefore he is not allowed to bring his wife into countries that adhere to Sharia Law. Two points of interest here:

1) I thought it interesting that two American Arabs at Blockbuster believe that our President is a Muslim, and

2) Who follows a strict Islamic creed. They also said that's the

reason he bowed to the King of Saudi Arabia. It was a signal to the Muslim world, acknowledging his religion.

For further consideration, here is a response from Dr. Jim Murk, a Middle Eastern Scholar and expert on Islam. This is his explanation of what the Arab American's were saying.

"An orthodox Muslim man would never take his wife on a politically oriented trip to any nation which practices Sharia law, particularly Saudi Arabia where the Wahhabi sect is dominant. This is true and it is why Obama left Michelle in Europe . She will stay home when he visits Arab countries. He knows Muslim protocol; this includes, bowing to the Saudi King. Obama is regarded as a Muslim in the Arab world, because he was born to a Muslim father; he acknowledged his Muslim faith with George Stephanopoulus. Note that he downplays his involvement with Christianity, by not publicly joining A Christian church in D.C. And occasionally attending the chapel for services at Camp David . He also played down the fact that America is a Christian country and said, unbelievably, that it was one of the largest Muslim nations in the world, which is nonsense. He has publicly taken the side of the Palestinians in the conflict with Israel and he ignored the National Day of Prayer, something no other President has ever done.

He is bad news! He conceals his true faith to the detriment of the American people." --- Jim Murk, Doctor of Philosophy in Middle Eastern Culture & Religion.

Actions speak louder than words.

Another interesting item regarding Sharia Law

Why has Barack Hussein Obama insisted that the U.S. Attorney

General hold the trials of the 911 Muslim Terrorists in Civilian Courts as Common Criminals instead of as Terrorists who attacked the United States of America ?

If the Muslim Terrorists are tried in Military Tribunals, convicted and sentenced to death, by LAW, Barack Hussein Obama, as President of the United States , would be required to sign their Death Warrants. He would not be required to sign the death warrants if they are sentenced to death by a Civilian Court . Recently, Muslim Jihadist, Army Major Hassan slaughtered non-Muslim, soldiers at Ft. Hood , Texas rather than go to Afghanistan and be a part of anything that could lead to the deaths of fellow Muslims. He stated that Muslims 'could not and should not kill fellow Muslims.'

Is the motive for Barack Hussein Obama's insistence on civilian trials, to make sure he doesn't have to sign the death warrants for the Muslim Terrorists? Why would he, as President of the United States , not sign the death warrants for Muslim Terrorists who attacked the United States and murdered over 3,000 U. S. Citizens on 9/11? Could it be that he is forbidden by his religion to authorize the execution of Muslims?

Think about that! Open your eyes, ears and mind to who the President is, how he behaves and what he is doing.

SOMEONE WHO SUPPORTED OBAMA

Obama's ability to connect with voters is what launched him. But what has surprised me is how he has failed to connect with the voters since he's been in office.

He's had so much overexposure. You have to be selective. He was doing five Sunday shows. How many press conferences? And now people stop listening to him. He's lost his audience. He has not rallied public opinion. He has plunged in the polls more than any other public figure since we've been using polls. He's done everything wrong. Well, not everything, but the major things. I don't consider it a triumph. I consider it a disaster!? And that's what his friends are saying about him.

As the boy president occupied the White House on January 20, 2009 it was predictable that his presidency would last a year, at most, because the things he promised and the things he stood for were so uniquely un-American. Looking back over his year in office, any reasonably precocious fourth grader could make a cogent argument in opposition to nearly everything he's done. In fact, his policies have been so extreme and so far outside the mainstream that he was destined to achieve the most spectacular fall from grace of any American president in history. It was easy to see him serving out the final three years of his term as a virtual exile in the White House, afraid to venture out among any but the most rabid partisans.

Seeing his most ambitious initiative, healthcare reform, die in the flames of the Massachusetts Massacre, Obama made a hastily-planned "sortie" to Ohio for yet another Bush-bashing, self-aggrandizing stump speech on job creation. It was vintage Obama, full of left wing hyperbole and planted questions from the Kool-Aide drinkers in the hand-picked audiences, but there were just two things wrong with it: 1) almost everything he said was either wrong or an outright lie, and 2) he is so overexposed that no one in the television audience really wanted to see him.

Obama Kool-Ade drinkers in the media, and elsewhere, like to describe Obama as a very bright man, a true intellectual (compared to George W. Bush and Sarah Palin, of course)? If that is the case, why has he demonstrated such a great inability to learn from his failures? The strident words and the in-your-face attitude of his Ohio speech were proof that he has totally misread the meaning of the Scott Brown victory in Massachusetts.

Whatever hopes and dreams he had for his time in the White House, whatever grandiose plans he had for transforming the United States from a constitutional republic with a free market economy into a socialist dictatorship with a centrally planned economy, were all lost on Tuesday, January 19, 2010, one day short of a full year in office.

Yet, he appears to have learned nothing from the experience.

A comedian once asked, rhetorically, "Did you ever get the feeling that the world was a tuxedo and you were a pair of brown shoes?"? In the context of 21st century American politics, and assuming that he has any capacity at all for honest self-examination, Obama must be feeling today very much like a pair of brown shoes at a black tie soiree.

When a politically naive and totally inexperienced young black man, with a glib tongue and an exceptional ability to read words convincingly from a teleprompter, announced that he was ready to serve as President of the United States, Liberals and Democrats saw it as a perfect opportunity to expiate whatever white guilt they may have felt, which was apparently considerable among those on the political left. It didn't seem to bother them that, as one pundit has remarked, every time he walks into a room he is the least experienced and the least qualified man in the room? Nevertheless, his friends in the worldwide socialist movement and the international banking community figured out how to smuggle hundreds of millions of dollars in illegal campaign funds into the country, the black community rallied to his banner, and American Liberals and the mainstream media jumped on board the bandwagon. Together, they made it happen for him. But now, just one year later, Obama appears destined to become the unhappiest man in American politics, unhappier than even former Senator John Edwards, who runs a close second, and former president Bill Clinton.

Clinton will be the third unhappiest man because, after capturing the big prize, he frittered away whatever chance he had of ever being compared favorably with Franklin D. Roosevelt as one of the 20th century's greatest Democratic presidents. Not only was he a politician of unusual skill and insight, he was widely known as a policy wonk, among policy wonks, and he had the drive and the personal charm to be loved and respected around the world. Unfortunately, he was never able to put the public trust at the top of his priority list. Instead, he surrounded himself with a large cadre of trusted enablers who allowed him to conduct himself as if he were, not the President of the United States, but the class stud on an extended spring break in Acapulco.

Now that he's been out of office for nearly a decade and he's married to the current Secretary of State, he spends his days trying to find something useful to do without calling an undue amount of attention to himself. Having lied so shamelessly to the American people, having perjured himself in a court of law, having turned the Oval

Office into a sexual playpen, and having suffered the humiliation of impeachment, he's smart enough to know that he has little reputation left to protect. So in order to protect whatever legacy remains, he walks a tightrope every day, and he has many more years to walk it without falling off.

Former Senator John Edwards is destined to be the second unhappiest man in American politics because he will be known forever as the most thoroughly despised scumbag in the political arena. A trial lawyer, Edwards amassed a $60 million fortune by winning large jury awards against doctors, hospitals, and corporations. His specialty was cases in which children were born with cerebral palsy, which he blamed on doctors who had waited too long to perform C-sections, a claim that doctors and medical researchers have described as "junk science".? Then, like Obama, he decided that his experience in the courtroom, his glib tongue, and his one term in the U.S. Senate qualified him to be President of the United States. He entered the 2004 Democratic presidential primaries, raising an incredible amount of money for a newcomer to elective office, most of it raised illegally by bundlers, in plaintiff's law firms across the country. He was unsuccessful in his quest for the Democratic nomination but was selected by his Senate colleague, John Kerry, as his running mate.

Two years later, in 2006, Edwards met a young blonde film producer, Rielle Hunter, and embarked on a love affair with her. On February 27, 2008, Hunter gave birth to a daughter, for whom Edwards has consistently denied paternity, until now.

Taking into account that all of this was happening while his wife was waging a long battle with breast cancer, Edwards now has the well-deserved reputation of being the sleaziest of the sleazy. He is so universally despised that, if he is on the lookout for a friend, he might as well resign himself to getting a dog, or moving in with O.J. Simpson. Terry Moran, host of ABC's This Week, put it all in perspective. He said, "What's interesting to note is that Edwards' latest admission (that he is the father of Hunter's child) came while he was in Haiti. As if the people of that sad place didn't have enough problems.? Clearly, the one thing Clinton and Edwards share that places them near the top of our list is their sexual peccadilloes, a shortcoming that Obama does not appear to share with them, at least from what we know so far.

What we do know about Obama is that, since his teen years, he has been mentored by, gravitated toward, and surrounded by the most dangerous sort of America-hating socialists, communists, and Marxists, from Frank Marshall Davis and Saul Alinsky to Weather Underground terrorists Bill Ayers and Bernadine Dohrn, to Rev. Jeremiah Wright, George Soros, and countless radical left college professors.

What destines Obama for the top spot on the list of unhappiest American politicians, aside from the failure of his economic recovery program, the failure of his radical cap-and-trade proposal, his failed attempt to give labor bosses unprecedented power to intimidate blue collar workers, and his ill-fated attempt at healthcare reforms, is the fact that he carries on his shoulders the hopes and aspirations of every black child in America. It is unfortunate that, because he is so far outside the American mainstream, and because he carries so much hatred in his heart for the country he seeks to lead, his failures will be viewed by generations of black children, not as the failure of a black socialist attempting to bring down a constitutional republic, but simply as the failure of a black man.

A man can fail in the eyes of his countrymen and still be dearly loved by those closest to him. But in Obama's case, his wife and his two daughters will be there to suffer every agonizing step of his fall along with him. And for the rest of his life, each time he looks into their eyes, and into the eyes of black people everywhere, he will see the crushing disappointment that his ill-fated attempt at national transformation has caused them.

He will be the country's unhappiest man, living the rest of his life knowing that his daughters know that the whole world sees him as a failure. He is simply the wrong man, in the wrong job, in the wrong country, at the wrong time in history.

DEAR PRESIDENT OBAMA:

You are the thirteenth President under whom I have lived and unlike any of the others, you truly scare me.

You scare me because after months of exposure, I know nothing about you.

You scare me because I do not know how you paid for your expensive Ivy League education and your upscale lifestyle and housing with no visible signs of support.

You scare me because you did not spend the formative years of youth growing up in America and culturally you are not an American.

You scare me because you have never run a company or met a payroll.

You scare me because you have never had military experience, thus don't understand it at its core.

You scare me because you lack humility and 'class', always blaming others.

You scare me because for over half your life you have aligned yourself with radical extremists who hate America and you refuse to publicly denounce these radicals who wish to see America fail.

You scare me because you are a cheerleader for the 'blame America ' crowd and deliver this message abroad.

You scare me because you want to change America to a European style country where the government sector dominates instead of the private sector.

You scare me because you want to replace our health care system with a government controlled one.

You scare me because you prefer 'wind mills' to responsibly capitalizing on our own vast oil, coal and shale reserves.

You scare me because you want to kill the American capitalist goose that lays the golden egg which provides the highest standard of living in the world.

You scare me because you have begun to use 'extortion' tactics against certain banks and corporations.

You scare me because your own political party shrinks from challenging you on your wild and irresponsible spending proposals.

You scare me because you will not openly listen to or even consider opposing points of view from intelligent people.

You scare me because you falsely believe that you are both omnipotent and omniscient.

You scare me because the media gives you a free pass on everything you do.

You scare me because you demonize and want to silence the Limbaugh's, Hannitys, O'Reillys and Becks who offer opposing, Conservative points of view.

You scare me because you prefer controlling over governing.

Finally, you scare me because if you serve a second term I will probably not feel safe in writing a similar letter in 8 years.

FROM A FRIEND WHO WORKS AT THE KENNEDY SPACE CENTER:
Thought you all might like to know what the "visit" from the President to the workers at the Kennedy Space Center was really like.

The day before the meeting, a 747 landed and unloaded 6 limousines and a small army of his security staff. They drove 3 miles to the building where he would be, checked it out, then turned around and drove back and got into the 747 and left.

(Your tax dollars at work). The meeting was held at one of the smallest buildings on KSC. All the staff in this building were told to stay home and not come to work. Then only 40 guests were invited to hear him speak. All dignitaries and VIPs and not one, I repeat not one, worker from all those that work hands on and actually with the shuttle were invited. It was so staged and phony, it just makes my blood boil.

Then that man said he wants to land on an asteroid!!!! Idiot. Here he is giving the Space Station to the Russians who want to charge us 100 million dollars per seat to fly one of our astronauts to the Space Station. Rumor now has it that the last mission also may be canceled. We really feel so bad for the workers out there; some are still raising families and have bills to pay. From the time his 747 landed to the speech given to the VIPS and return to take off was about 90 minutes. He was in a hurry to get to Miami where Gloria Estefan was having a rally for the Cubans and fund raising for Democrats.

So there you have it. I will leave you with your own conclusions. I sure have mine.

OUR EUROPEAN ARROGANCE IN ALPHABETICAL ORDER

The American Cemetery at Aisne-Marne, France - total of 2289

The American Cemetery at Ardennes, Belgium - total of 5329

The American Cemetery at Brittany, France - total of 4410

Brookwood, England American Cemetery - total of 468

Cambridge, England - 3812

Epinal, France American Cemetery - total of 5525

Flanders Field, Belgium - total of 368

Florence, Italy - total of 4402

Henri-Chapelle, Belgium - total of 7992

Lorraine, France - total of 10,489

Luxembourg - total of 5076

Meuse-Argonne - total of 14246

Netherlands - total of 8301

Normandy, France - total of 9387

Oise-Aisne, France - total of 6012

Rhone, France - total of 861

Sicily, Italy - total of 7861

Somme, France - total of 1844

St. Mihiel, France - total of 4153

Suresnes, France - total of 1541

Apologize to no one.

Remind those of our sacrifice and don't confuse arrogance with leadership.

The count is 104,366 dead brave Americans.

And we have to watch an American elected leader who apologizes to Europe and the Middle East that our country is "arrogant"!

How many french, Dutch, Italians, Belgians and brats are buried on our soil, defending us against our enemies?

We don't ask for praise ... but we have absolutely no need to apologize!!

Please---- do not delete, do think about this.   Thank you.

I hope you remember this when election time comes around again.

THANK YOU!

BRYAN CLARK